Loose Ends

A comedy

Frank Vickery

Samuel French — London
New York - Toronto - Hollywood

LOOSE ENDS

First performed at the Sherman Theatre, Cardiff, by the Sherman Theatre Company, on 28th April, 1994, with the following cast:

Marlene	Menna Trussler
Roy	Brian Hibberd
Bev	Donna Edwards
Darren	Ian Staples
Louise	Kay Williams

Directed by Phil Clark
Designed by Jane Linz Roberts
Lighting by Keith Hemming
Sound by Andy Pike

COPYRIGHT INFORMATION

CHARACTERS

Marlene
Roy, her husband
Darren, their son
Louise, their daughter
Bev

ACT I

A caravan site on the Gower

Saturday

A shabby looking caravan is positioned slightly off C. *The front end faces the audience. It is the type of van which has two doors — one that leads directly into the lounge and another into the kitchen. The front and downstage side of the van is cut away, allowing us to see the interior of the kitchen and the lounge. We can see benches, table, table seat, cupboards, television, gas lamps, cooker, sink, etc. There are entrances and exits through the kitchen and lounge into the bedroom of the van. The bedroom cannot be seen*

Four chairs, a barbecue and an upturned milk crate — which acts as a table — are positioned C, *just outside the lounge door*

When the Lights come up there is no-one on stage. It is a bright, sunny morning. The Lights change as the day gets older. The birds are singing and we hear the crash of waves not too far away. After a moment a car is heard approaching; it pulls up twenty or so yards away, the engine stops and three car doors slam

Marlene (*off*) Is this it? (*Calling*) Hallo? Bev?

Marlene rushes on and sees the caravan

Oh my God, Roy, get a look at this.

Roy enters. He is carrying a twelve-pack of lager and a newspaper

Marlene Bev said it was nothing posh, but this can't be it, sure to God. What do you think, Da? Where the hell is Darren now?
Roy He's locking the car. Wait till he gets to see this.
Marlene If I'd known it was this rough we could have brought the dog. Where's Darren with our bags?
Roy (*peering in through the window of the caravan*) I don't think there's anyone in.

Marlene I said we'd be here Saturday morning eleven o'clock. She's gone down the shop, I s'pect. (*She stands back to take a broader look*) God, it's not up to much, is it?

Roy How the hell we going to get in?

Marlene I don't know. (*She goes to the kitchen door and tries the handle. It opens*) Oh, it's not locked.

Roy Hey, taking a chance, in't she?

Marlene Not really, there's bugger all to pinch in there by the look of it.

Marlene and Roy step into the van. Marlene looks up at the gas lights, then at the two-ring gas cooker

Oh ... God!

Roy It's like stepping into the bloody sixties. (*He sets the lager down on the floor behind the table seat*)

Marlene Well it's only for the night — we'll be going home tomorrow.

Roy Imagine a fortnight here.

Bev enters, R. She has just returned from the shop and is carrying a loaf of sliced bread. She spots the open door and rushes in

Marlene (*looking out through the front window*) Where the bloody hell has Darren got to?

Bev (*delighted*) So you made it.

Roy Hallo, love. (*He sits at the kitchen table with his back to the lounge and opens his newspaper*)

Marlene Oh there you are, Bev.

They embrace

There's nice to see you.

Bev Just popped to the shop. Found it all right, did you?

Marlene Well, we did get lost, but that was Darren's driving and Saturday morning traffic — nothing to do with your directions, they were marvellous, weren't they, Roy?

Roy Very good, love, yes. (*He opens a can of lager and drinks*)

Marlene (*looking at her watch*) What's it now ... quarter to twelve. We did it in about two and a half hours. That's not bad going, is it?

Bev Darren brought you then.

Marlene Yes, but in our car see 'cause — (*meaning Roy*) he's still got another ten months to go on the — (*mouthing it, silently*) ban.

Bev (*laughing*) I'd have fetched you if you'd said.

Marlene Lover-boy wasn't doing anything. He'd only be in bed otherwise... but do you know, the minute I mentioned to him yesterday that you were going to be down here he was up like a lark and insisted on bringing us down here himself. I'n' that right, Roy?

Roy just looks

Hey, I was just saying now Bev, you've got a lovely van. It's beautiful with you, love. Beautiful!

Bev You've got to rough it a bit.

Marlene Yes. (*She sits down on a bench seat*)

Pause

Listen, you're not rushing back now, are you? You'll spend a couple of hours with us.

Bev (*sitting as well*) You don't want me hanging around.

Roy starts looking at the television on the floor near the kitchen table

Marlene Oh you know me — the more the merrier. And he's not much company, see.

Roy How does the telly work, Bev?

Bev Off a car battery by the door there, Roy.

Roy gets up and takes the television over towards the battery. During the following he tries to connect it up and get it working

Marlene Thank God for that, or that'll be him in the betting shop. If he can't watch his horses on a Saturday afternoon he's like a lump of hell. Hey, stay — company for me.

Bev (*going to the kitchen*) Well all right, as long as I'm home by six.

Marlene (*following her, more worried than curious*) You haven't got a date have you?

Bev No no, nothing like that.

Marlene stares at her, waiting for an explanation

(*Laughing*) I just have to be home, that's all.

Marlene Well I dare say you've got your reasons. Far be it from me to interfere.

Bev Let me show you round.

Marlene You got a life of your own, love, and you're not answerable to anyone.

Bev This is the kitchen, obviously.

Marlene If you got something you want to keep to yourself, it's up to you entirely.

Bev (*gesturing to the seating under the main window*) This makes up into a double bed ——

Marlene I mean why should you show anyone your business?

Bev (*pointing to it*) The table collapses and two can sleep there, plus two in the back bedroom.

Marlene If you don't want to tell me that's fine, love — I respect your privacy.

Bev Toilet and showers are at the other end of the field.

Marlene So it's not a fella then?

Darren enters R. He is carrying Marlene's beach bag and a suitcase

Bev (*smiling*) Did you get any of that or shall I go through it again?

Marlene (*laughing*) No no, I got everything — loud and clear.

Darren (*entering the van*) Oh ... So this is the mobile home with all the creature comforts, is it?

Marlene (*rushing to meet him*) Shut your mouth, Darren — Bev's given us this for nothing.

Darren (*putting the bag and suitcase just inside the bedroom*) Oh well in that case it's very nice, Bev. (*To Bev*) Don't forget to tell her where you keep the spare gas mantles.

Marlene (*laughing; making light of it*) Take no notice, Bev — he's only jealous. The only property he's ever owned is the fish tank in the front room.

Bev (*pointing to a drawer*) I always keep two spare mantles in here.

Darren Oh, so it *is* gas, is it? I was only messing about. (*He laughs*) I suppose the toilet's a hole in the ground somewhere, is it?

Bev I did say it was nothing grand.

Marlene Oh it's fabulous, love — fabulous and we're very grateful. Aren't we, Roy?

Roy (*banging the top of the television*) How do you get colour on this, love?

Bev It's a black and white set.

Marlene laughs then stops, slightly embarrassed. Pause

Marlene (*breaking the silence*) Let's have a nice cup of tea, is it?

Bev I'll get the water.

She passes Darren to go outside. The water container is kept in the top step of the caravan, along with a bag of charcoal

Marlene (*after Bev has disappeared*) Now look, I know this isn't the Ritz, right ——

Darren Well if that's you settled, I'm off back home.

Marlene No! No you can't go yet, boy. Stay and have some dinner first.

Darren But I want to be home by half-six.

Marlene (*coaxing*) Go on, stay mun. You can go home the same time as Bev then — in a convoy, like. Just in case one of you has a bit of trouble.

Darren Like what?

Marlene (*improvising madly*) She er ... she said her clutch was slipping all the way down here yesterday.

Darren When did she say that?

Marlene Two minutes before you came in.

Bev goes back inside the van with the bottle of water

Right, that's settled then. Dinner for four. Fish and chips all right for everyone? I won't ask him 'cause that's all he'd live on if I'd let him. Now then, Darren, go down the shop and get four fish and chips and a bottle of pop.

Darren I don't know where the shops are.

Marlene Bev will show you, I'm sure. Go on and don't forget now ... I don't want dandelion and burdock.

Darren and Bev go outside. Marlene remains in the kitchen. She stands in front of the cooker with a tea-towel in her hand. Pause.

Bev Follow me then.

Darren Listen, I can have a look at it for you if you like.

Bev (*smiling*) Pardon?

Darren Perhaps I can adjust it for you.

Bev What?

Darren It doesn't always mean you have to have a new one, see.

Bev (*laughing*) What are you on about?

Darren Your clutch. It's slipping, i'n'it? That's what the old girl said, anyway.

Bev Did she now.

Darren So what do you think?

Bev Yeah all right. (*Almost under her breath*) You can look under my bonnet any time. (*Louder*) Come on, let's go to the shop.

Darren makes to go off R

No, not that way. It's over by the pond. There's only a load of old blackberry bushes over there.

They both start to walk off in the other direction

You haven't seen the pond, have you? I'll show it to you on the way back.

They exit

There is a pause. The Lights change to indicate a passage of time

The television is now working and Roy is watching the climax of a race. The kettle is on

Marlene (*referring to the cooker*) I don't know ... this thing will take two hours to boil an egg.

Roy (*at the television*) Come on, come on ... (*He starts to jerk backwards and forwards, matching his movements to his horse. As the horse gets nearer the winning line, so the gyrating gets bigger and bigger*)

Marlene (*butting in*) For God's sake, Roy what you doing? You'll have the caravan on its side if you carry on.

Roy (*ignoring her*) Yes ... go on, yes. Go on. (*He gets louder*) Go on! Yes! Yes! *Yes*! YESSS!

Marlene (*joining in*) Yesss! You should have put a pound on that for me.

Roy It's the two thirty *I've* had a flutter on. I didn't have nothing on that, mun.

Marlene (*beginning to lay the table*) Nice girl, i'n' she? Bev.

Pause. Roy marks up the racing section of his newspaper

Darren have taken a shine to her, I can tell. I was going to try and pair them up together, but I don't know, they seem to be doing all right without any help from me. She's keen too, mind. I could tell that the minute she clapped eyes on him. He's not a bad-looking fella, mind ... I don't know where the hell we had him from, do you?

Roy Well he's my side of the family, i'n'he.

Marlene Oh is he?

Roy Well ay, he's a Morgans right through, that boy.

Marlene Oh there you are then. You can say what you like, ignorance is a wonderful thing.

Pause

Hey, it's just dawned on me. I've come down this weekend for a little break before I start my ... you know. *I* haven't stopped and *you* haven't shifted your arse yet.

Roy I'll wash the dishes.

Marlene I'm going to hold you to that too mind, 'cause sure as hell there's no dishwasher here. Dishwasher? It was all I could do to put my hands on a box of matches. It's supposed to be a six berth, I haven't found six of nothing yet.

Pause

Roy What time we eating, sweetheart?

Marlene Well as soon as they come back, i'n' it? I mean, we can't start without them, can we?

Pause. Marlene joins Roy on the long seat under the window

Hey, what's happening now on Monday?

Roy (*reading his newspaper*) How do you mean?

Marlene Well are you taking me or what?

Roy To hospital?

Marlene No, the south of bloody France. Where else am I going on Monday?

Roy I can have a day off, no problem.

Marlene Lover-boy have offered to take me, but I don't think it's his place. And I won't be very good after from what I can gather ——

Roy And you'd rather be sick on my lap than on any bugger else's?

Marlene Well if you want to put it like that, yes.

Pause

If I have a bad reaction they might want to keep me in for a couple of hours ... but that depends on the bed situation. That's why I'm keen on fund-raising for the Macmillan one. There's never enough to go round. (*Suddenly, she is very serious*) You will be there for me now, Roy, won't you?

Roy What do you fancy in the two forty-five?

Darren and Bev enter L with fish and chips, drinks, etc.

Darren (*handing Marlene the fish and chips through the dining area window*) Here you go.

Marlene Dinner won't be long now. Just waiting for the kettle to boil. (*She puts the fish and chips in the oven*)

Darren sits down in one of the chairs outside the van and tries to open the bottle of pop

Bev Everything all right in there?

Marlene Oh it's fabulous love, fabulous.

Bev I'd have given you a hand but I know what it's like.

Marlene (*coming out of the kitchen door*) Listen love, there's no room in there for me and my shadow let alone anyone else.

Bev Managed all right though, did you?

Marlene Fine love, fine. How about you and ——

Marlene points towards Darren just as Darren looks over his shoulder at her. She almost gets caught out

—— do you know I can see the shop from here, you know. I still can't work out how you two took so long fetching pop.

Darren We didn't.

Bev There's a big fish pond over there — (*she points*) with an eighteen-inch carp in it. I wanted Darren to see it.

Marlene Oh ay.

Bev (*sitting in a chair next to Darren*) Well he likes goldfish, he said.

Marlene Oh he does ... but he's going to have to settle for a bit of cod with his chips today. (*She laughs*)

Darren Have I got time to go to the toilet?

Marlene Dinner'll be ready in two minutes, mind.

Marlene goes back into the van and gets the fish and chips out of the oven. Darren makes to go off L in the direction of the toilet

Bev Hey Darren, you can go in the blackberry bushes if you like. I usually do.

Darren Oh all right.

He turns and exits R behind the van

Marlene You coming in, Bev?

Bev Er, no. I think I'll hang on.

Marlene (*putting fish and chips on two platters*) Just as well you said you'd wait for Darren though, Bev, 'cause I could only find three knives and forks here.

Bev I said you'd have to rough it.

Marlene Oh I'm not complaining ... it's just that if you'd said I could have fetched a couple of my own down.

Bev I'll be going home later — you won't have a problem then.

Marlene (*a little worried*) Course, you want to be home by six, don't you? Roy?

Roy looks up and Marlene gestures for him to come to the table. He goes to the table as she puts the rest of the chips back into the oven

Darren returns from the toilet. He goes straight into the van, wiping his fingers on the seat of his jeans

You'll have to wait for yours, boy. Me and your father will have to finish first.

Darren joins Bev back outside the van and sits down opposite her

(*Waving a tea-towel around*) Lot of flies down here, Bev. (*She picks up the net curtain to peer out of the kitchen window*) They all seem to be coming from the blackberry bushes behind the van.

Bev smiles, embarrassed

(*To Roy*) Nice bit of cod?

Roy doesn't answer. He takes a rather large bone from between his lips and shows it to Marlene

Oh shut up and put it on the side of your plate.

Darren (*to Bev*) What do you think about this idea of my mam's?

Marlene Do you think I'll be able to pull it off, Roy?

Roy What now?

Bev (*to Darren*) I've already told her ... she should wait till she's had all her treatment.

Marlene I know eighteen hundred pounds *sounds* like a lot of money ...

Roy I don't know what you're talking about.

Darren She's not going to listen, is she?

Bev Don't worry about it. She's going to feel pretty rotten for the next couple of months anyway.

Marlene But that's how much one of those Macmillan beds cost these days, see.

Roy Are we having a new bed?

Darren And after? How is she going to feel then?

Marlene A bit of a concert up the club shouldn't be too hard to organize, what do you think?

Roy produces another fish bone

Bev There's plenty of time yet. The trouble with your mother, Darren, is she doesn't realize how ill she is.

Darren She knows she's bad ——

Marlene And you'll help me out, won't you, Roy? You and the rest of the family, like.

Roy What can *I* do?

Bev She thinks chemotherapy is going to be a doddle ... the truth is she's going to have a rough time of it and she'll need all the support she can get.

Marlene Well I thought you could do a sponsored drink.

Bev All I'm saying is ... I know why she wants to do it. Most people want to show their appreciation and give something back, but there'll be plenty of time for that once she's had the all clear and we know she's out of the woods.

Marlene What do you say then, Roy? Do you agree to that or what?

Suddenly, Roy starts to choke

Now is that a yes or a no? Don't speak with your mouth full.

Roy makes a choking noise

Something gone down the wrong way?

Roy can't answer and is on the verge of panicking

Well drink something, for goodness sake.

Roy starts to make a funny noise

Darren, come quick, your father's choking!

Darren and Bev rush into the van. Darren furiously begins to beat Roy's back. Bev pushes Darren out of the way and attempts the Heimlich manoeuvre. They all freeze

Coloured pools of light flash on and off. Tom Jones sings "Boney Maloney"

Black-out

During the Black-out, Marlene and Bev exit

Darren and Roy clear away the table, moving everything to the sink unit and cupboard

Darren exits into the bedroom

Roy takes off his jacket and throws it on the long seat. He gets a tin opener and nail file and gets down on all fours to fiddle with the car battery

The Lights come up and the music fades

Marlene and Bev enter L. Both are wearing sunglasses, and Marlene is wearing a straw hat

Marlene This is a lovely site, Bev. I wouldn't mind buying a caravan down here myself. On the other side of the field though, of course, you know ... where there's 'lectric light, shower and toilet, extractor fan ... you know, that sort of thing. (*She sniffs*) Do you know, I can still smell that fish from dinner time, can you? It's a bugger to hang, mind, i'n' it?

Throughout the following scene, Roy continually tries to clear his throat. It becomes very irritating

Bev (*to Marlene*) There's a show area just behind the shop. There's always one or two vans there for sale. I'll take you over later on if you like.
Marlene (*moving outside*) Oooh what? Wouldn't I.

Roy makes a noise. During the following, he fiddles with the car battery

Marlene After we've had a cup of tea, is it?
Bev Fill the kettle then and *I'll* make it.
Marlene (*going into the van*) Are you having any luck with that?
Roy Not much.
Marlene Oh God! And there's me telling Bev you can fix anything. (*She lights the gas under the kettle*)
Roy I'd stand a chance if I had some decent tools. I mean there's not a lot you can do with a bottle opener and a bloody nail file.
Bev You sit down, Marlene, I haven't done anything since you've been here.
Marlene (*going to the lounge door*) It's only tea, what's the matter with you?
Bev Never mind I'm doing it ... then I'm going to make tracks if I want to be home by six.
Marlene (*joining Bev outside*) Oooh hey — you haven't seen our Darren, have you?
Bev (*taking a tube of sun-tan lotion out of her bag*) He said something about the beach ... I don't know if he went.

Marlene (*sitting next to Bev*) Why didn't you go with him then?
Bev He didn't ask me. (*She rubs some lotion into her arm*)
Marlene That's our Darren all over, that is. He's exactly like him by there.

Roy is still clearing his throat

If you don't put it on a plate for 'em they don't eat it. Know what I mean?
(*She winks at her*) Perhaps you didn't fancy the beach though, did you?
Bev I didn't mind.
Marlene Honest to God. He's as thick as two planks sometimes. (*She takes the tube off Bev and helps herself*)

Roy makes another noise

Bev Perhaps he doesn't like me, Marlene.
Marlene Nonsense ... He haven't stopped talking about you since our Louise got married.

Roy looks at her and clears his throat

And I know for a fact he's rung you several times and you haven't been there.

Roy clears his throat even louder

For God sake, Roy — will you stop making that noise, you're driving me up the bloody wall!
Roy (*shouting*) I can't help it, there's something stuck in my throat.
Marlene (*shouting back*) Well eat a bit of bread then.
Roy (*shouting louder*) I have — it won't shift.
Marlene (*shouting*) It's a fish bone I s'pect.
Roy (*shouting*) No it's not a bone.
Marlene (*shouting louder*) How do you know?
Roy (*louder still*) 'Cause it don't feel like a bone.
Marlene (*screaming*) I'm telling you. It's a bone from that cod you had dinner time!

Roy gives up — he ought to know better than to argue. Marlene puts her legs up on a nearby chair. Pause

Hey Bev ... I was telling Roy earlier on ... I'm going to go for that bed.

Bev looks at her

You know, the Macmillan one. I'm sure I can raise the money.

Bev You don't have to do it.

Marlene Oh I know that ... but I *want* to.

Bev There's plenty of time, you don't have to do it yet.

Marlene But it's needed now, i'n'it?

Bev I'm beginning to wish I'd never said anything.

Marlene Oh I thought about it before you brought it up. I heard it mentioned more than once when I was in hospital. I said then I was going to do something and I am.

Bev That's fair enough but ... get through all your treatment first.

Pause

Marlene Are you trying to tell me something by here?

Bev No, I just think ——

Marlene If you know something I don't I think now's the time to say.

Bev There's nothing.

Marlene What about you, Roy?

Roy (*going to the lounge door with his newspaper*) What?

Marlene Are you hiding something from me?

Roy Like what?

Marlene I don't know. I don't want no secrets, mind. If there's anything going on with me I want to know about it. (*To Roy*) Right? (*To Bev*) Right?

Roy sits at the top of the lounge door steps

Bev You're barking up the wrong tree as usual again, Marlene. All I'm trying to tell you is not to rush things. The next couple of months ... well ... they're not going to be a piece of cake for you.

Pause

Marlene You don't get it, do you? I wouldn't expect him to, but I thought better of *you*.

Darren enters from the bedroom

Oh there you are.

Darren Right, I'm off home then.

Marlene What?

Darren I want to be back by half six.

Marlene Bev was just going to make a cup of tea.

Bev (*standing*) That's all right, Marlene. I'll go the same time as Darren.

Marlene But you can't go yet ... either of you.

Darren Why?

Roy innocently clears his throat

Marlene (*improvising*) Because ... because ... because you're going to have to take your father to the hospital.
Roy What?
Marlene There's something stuck in his throat and he'll have to have it out.
Darren Is that right, Dad?
Marlene Make that noise for him, go on. Make that noise you've been making all afternoon.

Roy looks a bit nonplussed but complies

There you are see? If that's not a fish bone, nothing is.
Darren I don't know where the nearest hospital is.
Marlene Bev knows I'm sure.
Bev Singleton, I think.
Marlene There you are, Singleton. Take him quick now Darren, before it swells and closes his windpipe.
Roy I don't think there's any need ——
Marlene (*interrupting*) Shut up, Roy. I know what I'm doing.
Bev Perhaps if I have a look at it.
Marlene (*going to Bev*) Look, I know you're a nurse, Bev, but with all due respect, love ... I won't rest till he's been looked at proper like. And with me being bad with what I've got, I don't want nothing happening to him as well. You understand me, don't you?
Bev I think I'm beginning to, Marlene.

Pause

Right, well I'll be making my way back home on my own then.

Bev makes for the kitchen door but Marlene rushes around her and takes her DL. Darren sits on a step next to Roy

Marlene Well I'm glad you brought that up actually. I was going to ask you a favour. I know you got plans for tonight — and I don't want to know what they are — it's your business and it's up to you entirely, but ... I thought perhaps you'd stay by here with me until they get back from the hospital. I don't want to be on my own see. And I can't go with them 'cause I'll be in there myself on Monday and to be honest with you the thought now is just about turning me.
Roy (*pointing to his throat*) Marlene, I'm sure I can swill it down with ——
Marlene (*firmly*) Shut *up*, Roy!

Pause

What do you say, Bev? Can you help me out or what?

Pause

Bev Well I'm going to have to make a phone call then.
Marlene Cheers love, I owe you one.
Darren *I* had plans for tonight as well.
Marlene Good God, I'm sure they're not going to miss you down that snooker hall for one night.
Darren Who said I was playing snooker?
Marlene You make a phone call as well then. Got ten pences? Or shall I have a look for some?

Darren gives Marlene a look before exiting, L. *Bev exits* R

Marlene and Roy watch them go. Pause

Roy Marlene. Is there something going on here or what?
Marlene (*leading Roy into the van and towards the bedroom*) You go with Darren down that hospital, right? And I don't want to see either of you back here until at least ten o'clock.
Roy What!

They exit into the bedroom

There is a crossfade. Two small pools of light come up on either end of the stage

Bev steps into one and Darren into the other. They each hold a telephone receiver

Darren (*into the phone*) Yeah, can I speak to ——
Bev (*into the phone*) Can I speak to Philip, please.
Darren Julie?
Bev Philip?
Darren Darren.
Bev It's Bev.
Darren I'm all right.
Bev And you?
Darren Listen, you're not going to believe this ——
Bev I'm stuck down the van.

Darren There'll be other Saturdays ——
Bev It's true, I'm stuck down the van ——
Darren Well, still tonight but, it'll be late ——
Bev No don't come down ——
Darren 'Cause I don't know what time I'll be home ——
Bev No of course I haven't ——
Darren Haven't got a girl down here ——
Bev I just have to stay while ——
Darren While I take my old man to the hospital ——
Bev Don't be like that, we're going to have to do it another time ——
Darren What about one night in the week?
Bev All right, don't shout ——
Darren Honest to God I'm telling you the truth ——
Bev No I'm not lying!
Darren Don't hang up!
Bev Don't you *dare* hang up!

Suddenly we hear the noise of the dial tone. Bev and Darren return their
receivers. The dial tone sound stops, and there is a lighting change. Darren
and Bev wander C *until they're almost next to each other. They look up*

Darren Everything all right?
Bev Fine. You?
Darren Piece a cake.

Darren heads to the kitchen door and exits into the bedroom

The Lights change back to their previous state

Marlene enters from the bedroom and comes outside through the lounge
door

Marlene It's very nice of you to help me out, Bev.
Bev (*suspiciously*) You haven't planned any of this, have you, Marlene?
Marlene What do you mean?
Bev (*sitting*) I get the feeling you're doing an *Oklahoma* here.
Marlene Sorry love, I'm not with you.
Bev (*singing*) "Everything's going your way".
Marlene (*laughing*) Don't tell me it's not going yours as well.
Bev I knew it. Is Roy in on it too?

Pause

Marlene In on what?

Bev You may as well admit it, Marlene.

Marlene (*turning and walking away from her*) I don't know what you're talking about, love.

Bev Look me straight in the eye then and tell me you haven't deliberately done anything to keep me *and* Darren down here longer than we'd planned.

Marlene Well I can't deny I'm not aware of the way things are going ... and I can't deny I'm not glad about them either ... but you don't honestly think I had anything to do with Roy swallowing a bone, do you?

Bev Providing he *has* swallowed a bone.

Marlene He's not involved in anything to do with you and Darren, and neither am I. I swear to God it's kismet.

Bev What's that?

Marlene Fate, love, fate.

Roy enters from the bedroom, goes to the lounge and picks up his light coat

And you don't need any more than that. It's written in the stars and there's nothing me or Roy can do to alter it ... not that we'd want to. You're like a daughter to us already, you know that ... and if I thought for one minute you didn't like our Darren ——

Roy (*at the lounge door*) Marlene! I've got to take a coat or what?

Marlene What the hell do you want a coat for in this weather?

Roy Well it might be a bit nippy if we can't come back till ——

Marlene (*bringing him down the steps and leading him* DR) You go down that hospital now, right? And make sure you have an X-ray on that throat and anything else they're prepared to give you. I don't want you coming back here till they've told you you're A-One ... And I don't care how late it is. Like I said. Earlier on.

Marlene looks at Bev, who is still not totally convinced she's not up to something. Marlene smiles and laughs rather uncomfortably. Pause

Bev Well I don't know if it's me. I don't know if it's you, Roy. It could even be Darren ... but somebody somewhere is being taken for a ride.

Roy Hey Bev. It's me, i'n'it? How the hell else am I going to get to the hospital?

They all laugh, Marlene the loudest

Bev runs into the van and exits into the bedroom

Marlene (*clipping Roy across the back of the head*) You very nearly went and spoiled the whole bloody caboodle then.

Roy (*clearing his throat*) When?

Marlene Then.

Roy What caboodle?

Marlene Things were going along very nice thank you very much and then you have to open your gob.

Roy What's going on? (*He clears his throat*)

Marlene Nothing. (*She moves away from him*)

Roy What I nearly spoil then?

Marlene Nothing.

Roy Something's up.

Marlene It's nothing.

Roy (*shouting*) Then why am I going to the bloody hospital? (*He clears his throat even louder*)

Marlene (*turning on him*) Keep that up much more and it'll be 'cause you've been found mugged and ditched in the corner of a caravan site.

Roy I only want to know what's going on.

Marlene You're better off in the dark. (*She moves away from him*) Believe me, we're all better off if you're kept in the dark. Honest to God!

Bev enters from the bedroom and heads for the lounge door

Pause

Roy They told me you might get a bit like this.

Marlene Who?

Roy The doctors.

Marlene Like what?

Roy Well, you know ...

Marlene Like what, Roy?

Roy Funny, like.

Marlene Funny?

Roy Odd. Strange.

Pause

Thing is though they said *after* you'd had your treatment.

Marlene picks up one of the chairs to throw at Roy but she stops when she notices Bev at the lounge door

Marlene Oooh, all right?

Bev nods

How's Darren doing?

Bev He's combing his hair.

Marlene Combing his hair. (*Calling towards the bedroom*) Darren!

Darren (*off*) What?

Marlene Come and take your father to the hospital, he's desperate to go.

Darren (*off*) All right, mun.

Marlene (*to Roy*) Well you are, aren't you?

Bev (*to Roy*) It's still bothering you then, Roy?

Roy looks at her

Whatever it is in your throat?

Marlene Course it is. I mean it's not natural to keep making that noise all the time, is it.

Bev Funny, I haven't heard him do it for a while.

Marlene looks at Roy. He gets the message and makes the noise

Marlene Sounds a lot worse to me now, you know.

Bev I hope they won't keep you in, Roy.

Roy (*shocked*) What?

Marlene (*jumping in*) No they won't do that ... will they?

Bev Who's to say. (*She sits*) Look at the Queen Mother. They kept her in for nearly a week.

Marlene (*crossing to Roy*) Thank God I made you change your pants and vest this morning.

Roy But I've got the same ones ——

Marlene What?

Roy Nothing.

Bev They might want to keep you in overnight for observation.

Roy That's it, I'm not going. I'm not spending any week in no hospital.

Darren enters from the bedroom and walks outside via the lounge door

Marlene (*laughing*) She's was only having you on. Trying to put the wind up you, weren't you, Bev?

Darren Right, come on, let's have you then.

Marlene Go on now, Roy. The quicker you go the quicker you'll come back.

Roy But you said ——

Marlene Never mind what I said — just go with Darren now and everything will be all right ... I'm sure. (*She pushes Roy in the direction of the car*)

Roy I meant what I said mind, I'm not staying in.

He exits

Darren They won't keep him in will they, Mam?

Marlene Good God, not with a fish bone, no. Drive careful now, boy. And don't worry about me and Bev, we'll be all right here now till you come back.

Darren exits after Roy

Marlene (*turning to Bev*) He will be all right, won't he — Roy?

Bev Without a doubt, Marlene ... although I'm sure it would have nothing to do with you if he isn't.

Marlene What do you mean now?

We hear the car starting up and pulling away

Bev (*going towards the kitchen door*) Well it would be that old thing that renders us all helpless, won't it. (*Half in and half out of the door, she holds up a plastic string curtain over her mouth*)

Marlene What's that?

Bev Kismet.

Marlene laughs, embarrassed, as she goes into the van and exits into the bedroom. Bev follows her

The Lights fade. Tom Jones sings "I'm Never Going to Fall in Love"

The Lights come up; it is now evening, and the gas lights in the van are on

Marlene enters from the bedroom carrying a bottle of wine and two empty glasses

As she passes the kitchen she closes the curtains behind the sink unit. She comes out of the van and sits at the makeshift table. She sets down the two glasses and pours herself a drink

Marlene (*calling to Bev*) It's lovely out here, Bev. Bring the salted peanuts out with you, love? They're in an ashtray on the sink unit. You can't miss it — it's a bloody big glass thing.

Pause

I can see why you like coming down here, Bev ... it's very peaceful ... if peaceful is what you're in to. Plenty of time to be peaceful when you're dead and buried.

Pause

Oooh, now I could do with a fag.

Pause

Soon as I've had my last dose of chemo treatment, me and Roy are off abroad somewhere. Only don't tell him mind 'cause he don't know yet.

Bev enters from the bedroom wearing a long wrap around skirt and a strappy top. She gets the peanuts and stands on top of the kitchen steps

I thought Benidorm ... or Magaloof, anywhere as long as its warm and noisy ... and lots of young people everywhere. (*She turns and sees Bev*) Oooh that's nice. I haven't seen that on you before.
Bev It's just something I knock around in.
Marlene Come on — come and have a glass of wine. (*She pours Bev a glass*)

Bev joins her at the table

Cheers.

Long pause

When you working next?
Bev Wednesday.
Marlene Wednesday?

Pause

Oooh. You won't be there on Monday then when I'm having my treatment.

Pause

Bev You're not worried, are you?
Marlene Worried? Me? Good God, no.

Pause

I just thought if you were there, like I'd pop down to the ward and see you, that's all.
Bev You're going to be all right, Marlene.
Marlene (*over-confidently*) Good God, yes, I know that.

Pause

What shift are you working on Wednesday?

Bev Days.

Marlene Days. (*She has an idea*) You could come for tea. I do a nice lamb
dinner on a Wednesday.

Pause

Bev I think Darren's courting, Marlene.

Marlene No he's not.

Bev Well he's seeing somebody.

Marlene No way. The only thing he ever goes out with is a snooker cue.

Bev I'm seeing somebody too.

Marlene (*disappointed*) Oh you're not. Don't tell me he was the one you had
to be back at the house for.

Bev doesn't answer

I know it's none of my business, love but I hope it's not the same bugger
who's been knocking you about.

Again, no answer

It isn't him, is it? Bev?

Bev He wants to move back in.

Marlene Far be it for me to tell you what to do, love, but don't do it. He's
no good to you, you know that deep down. (*She smiles*) Does he know
about Darren?

Bev (*smiling*) Know what about Darren?

Marlene Well, have you told him how you feel about him?

Bev I don't know. How do I feel about him?

Marlene Oh come on, Bev. He's only got to come into the room.

Bev We've only known each other two minutes.

Marlene Sometimes that's all it takes, love.

Pause

Bev It's important to you, isn't it?

Marlene How do you mean?

Bev Me and — Darren ... together.

Marlene I want to see him taken care of, yes.

Bev (*laughing*) You mean you want to get rid of him.

Marlene Yeah, perhaps I do. (*She sips her drink*)

Pause

Bev No, it's not that, is it, is it, Ma?

Marlene doesn't answer

Tell me what it is?

Marlene I just want to see him settled, that's all. All mothers want that for their kids. Louise now, she's off, up and running and I want to see Darren happy in the same way.

Bev He's only twenty-three, there's plenty of time for that.

Pause

Marlene Should anything go wrong — with me and this treatment ——

Bev Nothing's going to go wrong, Marlene.

Marlene No I know that ... but should something go wrong ... I just want to know everyone will be taken care of.

Bev Like who?

Marlene Well ... Roy ... Louise ... Darren and you.

Pause

Bev (*putting her hand on Marlene's arm*) I don't know why you're worrying.

Marlene Ah but you do, don't you. You can't have what I got and not do anything else.

Bev This time next year we'll all be back here down the van having a good old laugh.

Marlene Yes ... but I'm not taking any chances. The minute I've had my last dose of chemo, me and Roy will be on that plane boy, and off up into the sun.

A car is heard. Its lights are seen as it pulls up to park

Bev Somebody's coming.

Marlene (*checking her watch*) Good God, they're not back already, are they?

Bev You don't think he's courting, then? Darren.

Marlene Listen love, if there is anybody sniffing around, don't worry about it. I'll sort them out.

Bev You can't do that.

Marlene I can do anything I like, love. I've put pay to half a dozen girls of his before now.

Bev (*scornfully*) Marlene.

Marlene He ought to know better anyway than to pick up with somebody I didn't care for. I was the same with Louise, see. If I hadn't taken to Wayne she'd have never have married him.

Bev Wayne got your approval then?

Marlene Oh he's fabulous, love — fabulous. Soon as she brought him home I knew he was the one.

Louise (*off; calling*) Mam?

Marlene Who's that?

Louise (*off*) It's me. Louise.

Louise runs on wearing the shortest pair of jean shorts anyone would dare, and a white frilly sleeveless blouse

Marlene (*going to her*) Louise? Good God, what are you doing down here?

Louise I just thought I'd come down, that's all.

Marlene You're not by yourself, are you? Where's Wayne then?

Suddenly, Louise starts to cry

What's the matter?

Louise continues to cry

Tell me what's wrong.

Louise cannot answer

If he's laid a finger on you, as God is my judge, I'll swear I'll castrate the bugger!

Bev Take her in the van, Marlene. Give her a minute, she'll calm down. Perhaps it's got nothing to do with Wayne.

Marlene She wouldn't have driven all the way down here if he hasn't. (*She takes Louise into the van*) All right, love, don't worry. I'll sort it out, whatever it is.

Bev exits behind the van

Trust Roy not to be here now in a family crisis. Now where's Bev? She was behind me a minute ago.

Louise (*sitting*) Leave her where she is. I don't want her to see me like this.

Marlene (*sitting next to her*) Go on — we're all girls together, what's the matter with you?

Louise I don't want her to know about me and Wayne.

Marlene Look, you've had a tiff — it's nothing to be ashamed of.

Louise I don't want her to know, right?

Marlene Everybody has their ups and downs.

Louise Promise you won't tell her anything.

Marlene Now it's no good keeping it all to yourself, mind.
Louise Promise me.
Marlene Oh all right ... my lips are sealed.

Bev returns

I suppose you want to stay down the night now, do you?
Louise Well I'm not driving back home tonight.
Marlene No all right, you shall sleep down.

Bev walks into the van

Bev, where you been, love — I've been looking for you.
Bev I left you and Louise to have a chat. How are you now, Lou — all right?
Marlene Her and Wayne have had a tiff.
Louise Mam!
Marlene It's all right, it's only Bev — she's practically family.
Bev Everything's all right now though, is it?
Marlene I told her she can stay down now tonight. She can, can she?
Bev Yeah, there's plenty of room.
Marlene She can share with you. Me and Roy can have the other double and
    Darren — well he can kip anywhere.
Bev I wasn't staying down, Ma.
Marlene No, but you will though, won't you? Too late to go home now see,
    i'n'it? I'm going to finish my drop of wine. (*She mimes the word "you"*)
    — have a chat with — (*she mimes the word "her"*) while I'll go out by —
    (*she mimes the word "there". She steps outside the van and gestures for
    Bev to carry out her instructions*)
Bev You found us all right then?
Louise It wasn't easy, I couldn't see the signs — I cried all the way down here.

Marlene hides down next to the towbar

Bev Does Wayne know you're here?
Louise I don't think he cares.
Bev (*joining Louise on the long seat*) Nonsense, I bet he's worried sick.
Louise Well if he is he's only worried about how he's going to get home from
    the disco.

*On the word disco, Marlene pops her head up to look in the window only to
be spotted by Bev. Bev grabs Louise's hand in an attempt to distract her.
Marlene hides next to the tow bar again*

Bev Oh, you were having a night out then.

Louise His idea, I was quite happy to stay in and have an early night.
Bev But you two always hit the town on the weekends.
Louise We're married now — we've got to watch the pennies.
Bev Is that what it's all about then?

Louise shakes her head. Pause

Louise You being a nurse perhaps you can understand it.
Bev What?
Louise We've been married five weeks now ...

Pause; Bev waits patiently

He wouldn't leave me alone before I walked down that aisle.

Pause

One night — we were still on honeymoon and he couldn't ...
Bev What?
Louise You know. (*She wiggles her finger*) It's all right, I said — it's no big deal.
Bev And it isn't.
Louise Isn't it?
Marlene (*popping up in the window*) God no, it happens to your father all the time. (*She races back into the van and sits herself down in between Louise and Bev*) Now look, love ... let me tell you a thing or two about men. Basically they fall in two camps. I'm right, Bev, aren't I?

Bev looks uncertain; she doesn't know what Marlene's going to say

They can either do it ten times a day and in all conditions and positions ... or everything has to be just right. You know, an hour or two getting in the mood so that when it finally happens — (*she makes an exploding noise from the back of her throat*) it's like Mount Etna. He can only do it the once but boy neither of you are fit for anything after that. (*She thinks*) I don't know what category your father falls in ... He's like Colin Jackson between the sheets. He's up and off before you know it. (*She laughs*) I'm only joking.
Louise It's not just the sex thing.

A slight pause as Marlene looks at Louise and then at Bev

Bev Something happened at the disco?
Marlene You've been to a disco?
Louise He thinks he's such a stud.
Marlene Tell me what happened 'cause if he's messed around, mind ...

Louise He hasn't gone that far but you know what he's like. He just can't stop flirting with everyone.

Marlene Oooh hey, hang on a minute by here now. In fairness, he's always done that. He even flirts with me ... which is why I've always liked him so much. (*She laughs as she crosses her legs*)

Louise Well I'm not having it anymore.

Marlene You used to like him doing it.

Louise No I didn't.

Marlene Yes you did, you told me. He used to chat up all the girls and you thought that was great 'cause he was yours and they couldn't have him.

Louise Well they can have him now 'cause he wouldn't be any good to them anyway.

Marlene Look here, love. Wayne being like he is is what attracted you to him in the first place. You try and change him and you'll end up with someone who bears no resemblance to the fella you fell in love with.

Pause

Louise Did you change Daddy?

Marlene Good God, no. He's as big a slob now as when I married him ... but I wouldn't change him for the world, see.

Louise Being married *does* change things though.

Marlene Oh no it doesn't ... having kids does ... that's when it's a whole new ball game.

Pause

Look, Wayne's a tidy boy, right? He wouldn't do anything to hurt you 'cause he knows he'd have me to deal with. As for this flirting thing ... you're going to have to learn to live with it. I mean, what does it matter where he gets his appetite from as long as he comes home to eat, know what I mean? (*She laughs to Bev*)

Louise But we haven't had a "meal" together for ages.

Marlene Leave that to me. I'll have a word with him when I get home.

Louise Don't you dare.

Marlene I won't say you told me.

Louise How else would you have known? Don't say anything. Tell her not to say anything, Bev, you know what she's like.

A car is heard approaching. We see its lights as it turns to park

Bev You're better off not getting involved, Ma.

Marlene All right all right all right! I won't say a dicky-bird ... I'll just drop a few hints.

Bev There's somebody coming.
Marlene (*getting up to see*) I bet that's them.
Louise (*joining Marlene*) It could be Wayne.
Bev (*standing*) I thought he didn't know where you were.
Louise I might have screamed at him I was going back to my mother. He
could have had a mate bring him down.
Marlene I wouldn't hold your breath, love, that sounds like our banger
to me.

*The lights of the car are turned off and two doors are heard slamming.
Marlene and Bev position themselves outside the van. Louise sits in one of
the chairs*

Roy enters, quickly followed by Darren

Marlene I thought you'd have been back before now. How did it go?
Darren Don't give me that.
Marlene What are you talking about?
Roy Forget it, Marlene, the boy knows. (*He is pleased to see Louise*) What
are you doing down here, love?
Marlene Knows what?
Darren That it was all a wild goose chase.
Louise Oh Dad, it's Wayne, he's upset me awful.
Marlene Not now, Louise. (*To Darren*) What wild goose chase?
Darren If you wanted me to stay the night why didn't you come straight out
and ask me?
Roy (*to Marlene*) I haven't said anything, mind. He put it all together
himself. (*To Louise*) What's Wayne done, babes?
Louise Well ——
Bev Not now, Louise. Is that right, Marlene? Did you want him to stay the
night here?
Marlene (*to Bev*) Good God no. (*To Darren*) But if I did, and I'd asked you,
would you have?
Darren I don't know.
Marlene Well let's find out then, shall we?
Bev Marlene, you've been at it again. (*She sits on the steps*)
Louise The only man a girl can depend on is her ——
Darren (*shouting*) Not *now* Louise.

Roy goes into the kitchen and gets a can of lager

(*To Bev*) And don't pretend to be innocent. I bet you were in on it as well.
Bev (*standing*) Me?
Marlene Will you stay down here tonight?

Bev Don't flatter yourself — I can't wait to see the back of you.

Darren Well you haven't got to wait long.

Marlene Darren, will you answer me.

Bev (*shouting*) I didn't know what your mother was up to any more than you did.

Marlene (*shouting at Darren*) Do you hear me! Are you going to stay down here tonight, or what?

Darren (*shouting*) No!

Louise I'm going to have a word with Wayne and if he doesn't ——

All (*except Roy; screaming*) Not now, Louise!

Louise gets her hanky, sits and starts to cry

Marlene (*to Darren*) Give me the car keys.

Darren What?

Marlene The car keys — let's have 'em.

Darren But how am I going to get home?

Bev Have *my* car.

Marlene Bev!

Bev I don't care. Anything as long as he's out of my sight.

Marlene What you got — third party or fully comp?

Bev Third party. (*She sits on the far steps*)

Marlene Third party. (*To Darren*) Well that's it, you're not covered. Keys please.

Darren (*throwing her the keys*) Three hours I spent sitting in that hospital.

Roy (*coming out of the van*) That's a long time see, Marlene.

Marlene (*to Darren*) I wonder how much time *I've* spent there waiting for *you* over the years.

Roy True.

Darren I know why you did it. It's all part of your plan to get me and her together, isn't it?

Bev (*standing*) Hey, I've got a name.

Darren Well it's not going to work.

Bev Absolutely not.

Darren The time's come now when you've got to stop interfering, and not just in my life but in everybody else's as well.

Roy (*sitting in a chair next to Louise*) Fair comment.

Marlene Me, interfere?

Louise You know you do, Mam.

Roy She is right, Marlene.

Marlene Well thank you very much.

Bev I know you're only trying to do the right thing.

Roy And she is, ay.

Marlene (*to Bev*) So you're on their side as well, are you?

Darren It's not a question of sides.

Roy You're right, it's not.

Marlene Far be it from me to ——

Louise You've got to learn to let us get on with it, Mam.

Roy Hear, hear.

Marlene And where would you be if I told you that earlier on? If you want to be left to get on with it, my girl, you shouldn't have come running to me in the first place.

Bev She's got a point there, Louise.

Louise (*getting up and going to Bev*) Hark at you — you're not even family.

Marlene (*grabbing her*) Don't you speak to her like that.

Darren (*shouting*) Well she's not!

Roy (*shouting*) And don't you shout at your mother either.

Marlene She's just like one of my own.

Roy She is too.

Bev No I'm not, Marlene.

Roy Well perhaps not exactly like our own, you know.

Marlene She's got a damned sight more feeling in her than either of you two.

Roy So there you are!

Darren We all know what you're like and we all put up with it ...

Louise We've even laughed at it before now.

Darren But you've gone too far this time.

Roy Now he's got a point.

Marlene I haven't done anything to hurt anyone.

Darren You want too much.

Marlene I don't "want" for my kids any more than any other mother.

Roy And she don't.

Marlene If I overstep the mark it's because I try and "give it" to them.

Darren Even if they want something else.

Marlene The trouble with you is you don't bloody know *what* you want.

Roy Now that's a fact.

Darren I know I don't want you arranging my life for me.

Louise (*standing*) Or me.

Marlene Right! Well bugger off now then, the pair of you.

Louise There's no need to be like that.

Marlene Isn't there?

Roy You tell 'em, Marlene.

Marlene Look here, I know you're young and you think you know everything ... but the truth is you don't know bugger all.

A pause

(*Holding back tears; crocodile ones, though*) I'm going into that hospital on Monday and I don't know whether I'm going to come out of there.

Louise What?

Marlene I'm about to start treatment that's going to knock the shit out of me.

Pause

When Bev said I could have the caravan for a day or two I thought, oh that would be nice. I can have my kids around me and all the people I care for. (*To Louise*) But when I asked you what did I get? "Oh I'm sorry, Mam, but me and Wayne go out on a Saturday." (*To Darren*) I didn't even ask you because I knew I'd get a bloody big "No" and all the excuses under the sun ... but I thought if I could get you to bring us down here maybe I could con you into staying the night. I didn't think what I was hoping for was such a big deal ... maybe I did and that's why I lied.

Darren So getting me to stay down had nothing to do with Bev then?

Roy Course it didn't.

Marlene It's no secret I'd love to see the pair of you hitched up together ... but it seems the more I try to bring that about the less chance there is of it happening.

Bev So much for *Kismet*.

Marlene (*going to her*) Sorry, Bev, love. I didn't know what you'd say if I'd asked you to stay. I dragged you into all this because I was afraid to take the chance.

Roy (*to Bev*) Can't blame her for that see, can you?

Darren (*to Bev*) So you didn't have anything to do with it?

Bev Believe me, you're the last person I want to spend time with. I'm sorry, Ma, I'm going home. (*She heads towards the kitchen*)

Louise And me. You want a lift Da or what?

Darren (*referring to Bev*) I'm not travelling with her, that's for sure.

Marlene So you're all buggering off now and leaving me down here with your father.

Louise You told us to leave two minutes ago.

Marlene That's all right ... you go, my girl. You do exactly what you want and don't consider me at all ... just as long as you know from now on it cuts both ways.

Darren What do you mean?

Marlene It's my life I know, but it's just as easy for me to give up and give in.

Bev (*from the kitchen steps*) Marlene!

Marlene No — it's about time they heard it. Why should I fight. I wasn't doing it for me anyway, it was for them.

Bev You don't know what you're saying.

Marlene I was going to hang on in there 'cause who else is going to make his bed in the mornings?

Roy (*to Darren*) Are you listening to this?

Marlene Shut up, Roy. Who else is going to lend him a tenner till the end of the week?

Darren (*to Roy*) Are *you* listening?

Marlene Shut up, Darren. Who's going to sit her down and tell her everything's going to be all right. Or do her washing for her — or give her a cup of tea and calm her down when her and Wayne have had a ding dong? Who's going to do all that — can you answer me? Well it's not going to be me, you can be sure of that.

Louise You can't threaten us.

Marlene Shut up, Louise.

Darren But you can't.

Marlene It's no threat, love. I'm just taking a leaf out of your book. From now on I'm looking after number one!

Pause

Louise So what you're saying then ... ? You're not going to have your treatment?

Marlene That's about the size of it, Louise — yes. (*She sits down next to Roy*)

Darren Don't listen to her, Lou, she's bluffing.

Marlene Bluffing am I? Look here — why should I watch my hair fall out, eh? Why should I listen to people tell me how well I'm looking when I know I look bloody awful. I don't want to watch my skin sag and my colour go. I don't want to. (*To Louise*) Everything I've ever done I've done for you. (*To Darren*) And you.

Louise (*crying*) Oh ... Mam. (*She sits on the other side of Roy*)

Darren Don't fall for it, Louise.

Marlene One of these days you're going to wake up and I won't be here.

Darren Oh Jesus — here we go.

Marlene You won't know how much you've missed me till I'm gone.

Louise (*still crying*) Oh Mam!

Darren (*shouting*) Don't try and make me feel guilty, right? 'Cause it's not going to work.

Marlene (*standing*) Guilty? You don't know the bloody meaning of the word.

Darren You're the one to blame, not me. I'm off.

He exits, R

Marlene (*shouting after him*) Yes go — go on, the easiest thing in the world is to walk away.

He has gone. Pause

Louise He didn't mean it, Mam ... and you didn't either, did you?

Marlene I'm the one to blame he said. Did you hear him? What have I done, eh? What crime have I committed, I ask you. If wanting to see your kids happy and settled is against the law then yes, in that case I'm as guilty as hell ...

Louise Tell me you didn't mean it, Mam.

Marlene You're a big girl now, Louise.

Louise What's that suppose to mean?

Marlene (*grabbing her by the shoulders*) It means, if you want to be left to get on with it, that's exactly what you're going to be left to do! (*She pushes Louise aside and heads for the van. She is half-way across the lounge when she stops and shouts*) Roy!

Roy jumps out of his seat and follows Marlene into the van

Bev exits

Tom Jones sings "My Foolish Heart". The Lights change; it is a starry evening

Roy turns out the gas light in the kitchen before he and Marlene exit into the bedroom

Louise goes into the van, turns out the gas light in the lounge, takes a duvet from under a seat and snuggles down under it on the long seat by the window

It is an hour or so later when Bev enters R. She is singing along to the Tom Jones song and drinking from a bottle of wine. She comes C, kicks one of the chairs in temper, hurts her foot, hops around and lands on the floor

The music fades

Darren appears in the darkness from behind the van, R

He seems to be preoccupied with the night sky and he stumbles over some small stones near the path of the van. Bev sits up and sees him. Still on the floor, she reaches over to the peanuts, grabs a small handful and throws them in Darren's direction. This frightens him and Bev laughs

Darren Bev?

Bev I hope you didn't catch anything in the thorns. I heard you in the bushes. (*She giggles*)

He moves towards her

I thought you'd gone home in a huff.

Darren I went to the pub. What are you doing out here?

Bev It's too hot in there ... in every sense of the word.

Darren (*shouting towards the bedroom*) She hasn't cooled down then — the old girl? (*He laughs*)

Bev Sshhh! Hell hath no fury as a woman spawned.

Darren (*standing over her*) Don't you mean scorned?

Bev I know what I mean. (*She giggles*) That's clever that, isn't it? Hell hath no fury as a woman —— (*She giggles even louder*) What are you doing swaying around up there, love? Come and sit down here by me.

She reaches up and pulls him down on top of her. He is laying across her legs. They both laugh. Bev takes another drink from the bottle, then Darren takes it from her and helps himself. Pause

Darren I want to ask you something.

Bev (*laying outstretched before him*) Yes!

Darren I haven't asked you yet.

Bev Go on then.

Darren What made you ——

Bev (*stretching out again*) Yes!

Darren (*laughing hysterically*) How many of these have you had?

Bev Three.

Darren Glasses?

Bev Bottles. (*She reaches over and takes another bottle of wine which was left on the milk crate earlier in the evening*) Is that all you wanted to ask me, Darren?

Darren No ... I just wondered why you bought a van.

Bev I didn't. My aunty left it to me ... God bless her. I spent a lot of time down here when I was a child. I don't know why, I've always liked it.

Darren Don't you get lonely?

Bev Sometimes ... but I haven't got to be down the van for that.

Pause

Darren I had my own shed.

Bev What?

Darren Yeah — at the bottom of the garden. I built it myself out of rafters and a load of old zinc. I used to sit in it for hours, ay — listening to the rain. I used to sit on the floor with my arms wrapped round my damp legs picking the scabs off my knees.

Pause

Bev Any time you fancy sitting in my shed ...

Darren (*getting up on his knees*) Oh it's not the shed I miss. It's being ten ... or eleven, or however old I was. Everything was safe then ... secure, like. All I had to worry about was how to dry my conkers.

He realizes how funny that sounded and starts to laugh. Bev laughs as well, and they fall back down on the floor together. Slowly their laughter dies away and there is a moment between them

Bev (*sitting up*) If you want to ask me something else — anything — you can, you know.

Darren (*kneeling*) Like what?

Bev Well, you know ... (*She offers herself to him again*)

Darren I can't imagine what it would be like without her ... you know .... my mam ... without her.

Bev It might not come to that, Darren.

Darren The big C never goes away though, does it? You just learn to live with the threat.

Bev And your mother will learn. She might never forget but you will ... and your father, and Louise, you all will. People do. They have to.

Darren What makes you so wise?

Bev It's not wisdom, it's part of my job. I see it every day, don't I. (*She has another sip of wine*)

Pause

Darren Hey, who did you call earlier on? You know, on the phone. Who did you speak to?

Bev Just a friend. And you?

Darren I had a date. Nothing heavy, just seen her once or twice, that's all ... Male?

Bev What?

Darren Your friend. Was it a bloke?

Bev We used to live together. I threw him out a couple of weeks ago.

Darren Why?

Bev Your mother told me to. (*She laughs*) Advised me to ... He wants to move back in. We were going to get married.

Darren What happened?

Bev I made a list. I wrote all his bad points on a sheet of foolscap and his good points on a fag paper. I gave him his ring back. We still lived together like, you know .... but not long after that he started knocking me about.

Pause. Bev has another drink

Darren Oh ... So he had a lot of bad points ... you must have liked him.
Bev It was physical. He was good-looking. Not as good-looking as you, like,
    and already I regret saying that, but it's true ... It took me a long time to
    realize it was only his body I was in love with.
Darren Do you miss him?

She doesn't answer, and takes another swig of wine

    Like crazy.
Bev No no no no ... it was biological. (*She laughs*) God, I shouldn't have said
    that.
Darren Why not?

She doesn't answer

    Hey, maybe we can help each other out.

She looks at him

    I'm hungry as well ... biologically speaking. Here we are, two young
    healthy, hungry human beings. Are we strong enough to ignore the call of
    the wild?
Bev Are we drunk enough not to?

*Darren bangs his fist on his chest and makes a Tarzan noise. Bev shouts for
him to be quiet and he collapses over her again. There is a slight pause*

    Have another drink, love.

They both have another drink

    It's not very romantic though, is it? You know, two people fulfilling a
    physical need.
Darren We can dress it up a bit if you want?

She laughs

    We can light a candle, open a tin of beans, eat them on a table-cloth? I know,
    I've got just the trick. (*He tries to take a ring off his finger*)
Bev What are you doing?
Darren (*taking her hand and slipping the ring on her finger*) It's only my

silver buckle ring, right? But ... there you are. (*He laughs again*) Congrat-
ulations on your engagement.

Bev (*laughing as she puts her arms around him*) Oh God ... You're crackers.

Darren But is it romantic enough for you?

Bev I've always wanted to do it under the stars.

He throws himself on top of her but she immediately pushes him off

No no ... wait.

Darren What's the matter?

Bev Not in front of my aunty's caravan.

Darren Where then?

Bev Behind it, love. Come on ... follow me.

She grabs hold of him and they both run off, exiting behind the caravan

Bev (*off*) There we are ... here will do.

Darren (*off*) We can't do it here. We'll get sand everywhere.

Bev (*off*) Oh God, I've forgotten my cap.

Darren (*off*) I think your hair looks lovely as it is.

Bev (*off*) No, my Dutch cap. We can't do it without using anything. Have you
got anything in your wallet?

Darren (*off*) I haven't even got a wallet.

Bev (*off*) We're taking a terrible chance if we ... ooohh. (*Passionately*) Oooh
Darren ... Darren ... (*Very breathy*) Darren ...

Darren snores, off

Darren! Wake up!

Louise Good-night, Mam.

Marlene (*off; from the bedroom*) Good-night, Louise.

Louise Good-night, Dad.

Roy (*off*) Oh ... good-night, love.

Pause

Marlene (*off*) Bugger off, Roy!

There is a slap, off

Tom Jones sings, "I Can't Stop Loving You"

Black-out

ACT II

The same

Sunday

Tom Jones is singing "The Resurrection Shuffle"

The Lights come up. It is a bright, sunny morning. The Lights change as the day gets older. Louise enters, L. She stands DL and starts exercising to the song, which now emanates from a portable radio sitting on the top step of the lounge door. Roy appears from behind the van, R. He has a newspaper under one arm and he is carrying a toilet roll in the other. He sets the toilet roll down just inside the van door, does the top of his trousers up and adjusts himself. He sits in a chair at the milk crate table with a mug of tea. More mugs and a tea-pot are on a tray. Darren appears at the kitchen door. He has just got up and he squints his eyes to see who is outside. He goes to the radio and switches it off

Louise Hey, I was working to that.
Darren What time is it?
Louise Half-past ten.
Darren (*sitting next to Roy*) Is it that early?
Louise You got a nerve.
Darren I'm knackered, mun.
Louise (*sitting next to Darren*) How come you changed your mind and came back last night?
Darren What does it matter? (*He pours himself a mug of tea*)
Louise Couldn't hitch a lift I suppose?
Darren Look, I stayed the night — that's what the old girl wanted.

Pause. Louise picks up her mug

What did she say after I left?
Louise I think she's sticking to her guns.
Darren And this morning?
Louise Nobody've said a word. We all had tea and toast in total silence.

All three drink their tea simultaneously. Pause

Darren (*looking around*) Where is she now then?

Louise shrugs her shoulders

(*To Roy*) Do you know where she is? (*He hits Roy's paper with his hand*)
Oi!

Roy looks up

The old girl. Where's she gone?
Roy Search me. I haven't had a word out of her all morning.

Pause

Darren Well what are we going to do about it?
Roy You can do what you want — I like a bit of peace and bloody quiet, me.
Louise She didn't mean what she said last night, Dad, did she? She will have
the treatment, won't she?
Darren Course she will. She said a lot of things last night she didn't mean.
Roy When your mother's got something in her head ——
Darren Look, we're talking big stakes here, right? If she don't have that
treatment ——
Louise She's got to have it. We know that and she does.
Roy I don't want to put oil on the fire, but your mother hasn't got to have
anything, Louise.
Darren But you wouldn't agree to ——
Roy Her not having treatment? It's her decision, but.
Louise You mean you wouldn't talk her out of it?
Roy Oooh, think about this now, the pair of you, will you? When have I ever
been able to talk your mother out of anything?

Pause

Louise We'll get Bev on to her. If anyone can talk her round she can.
Darren Yeah, you can ask her when she comes back.
Louise It'll be better coming from you.
Darren I don't think so ... not after last night.
Roy For God's sake, get in there, what the hell's the matter with you?
Darren She's not going to do anything for me.
Louise She will, she fancies you something rotten.

Darren Do you think so? (*He thinks about it*) No, she hates my guts.

Roy That's always a good sign.

Darren What?

Roy If a woman hates your guts, it's either 'cause she hates your guts or because she fancies you something rotten.

Darren How do you tell the difference?

Roy (*about to answer then changing his mind*) Ask your sister.

Darren looks at Louise

Louise Sometimes you can't. You've got to be prepared to get it wrong. Girls often say no to dates when they really want to go, and vice versa. They hide their feelings by showing the opposite.

Roy Fellas do that as well, mind.

Darren Do they?

Roy Come off it — I've seen you look at Bev.

Darren It doesn't mean anything. It's only a look.

Louise Now you sound like Wayne.

Roy I can remember when I used to look at your mother like that.

Roy gazes out. Darren looks at him incredulously then shakes his head

Louise I don't know why you and Bev don't just stop playing games and start being serious with each other.

Darren Listen to you. You'd have us paired up and married before I'd have time to blink.

Roy She wouldn't — your mother would.

Darren Well I'm not being pushed into anything ... and not for anyone. Old girl or no.

Louise looks at him and smiles as though she knows better

I'm going to get dressed.

He exits into the bedroom

Pause

Louise Do you think they'll sort it out?

Roy Who?

Louise Darren and Bev.

Roy Well, ay.

Pause

Sort what out?

Louise Oh, Dad! (*She moves chairs to sit next to Roy*) What exactly will happen if Mammy refuses treatment?

Roy Nothing for a bit ... then ——

Louise (*getting up*) She didn't mean it, Dad. She couldn't, could she?

Roy Your mother can be very determined when she wants to, as you know.

Louise Yeah but with something like this ... She can't think much of you or us if she's prepared to do something like that.

Roy I think you're looking at it from the wrong end, love.

Louise Mammy knows we love her.

Roy She didn't last night.

Louise Well she's going to know it today. Come on — let's go for a walk and find her.

Roy We don't know where she is. She could be anywhere.

Louise Let's try anyway.

They start to leave

Bev enters UR, *running. She has been out jogging and has a towel around her neck. She sits breathlessly in one of the chairs*

Bev Off somewhere?

Louise You haven't seen my mother, have you?

Bev Not since breakfast, no.

Louise We're going to look for her. Any suggestions?

Bev You could try the beach.

Louise Right.

Bev Or the bus station.

Louise She wouldn't have gone home, would she?

Bev It's possible. What do you think, Roy?

Pause

Roy I don't know.

Pause

Louise Walk on ahead, Dad — I'll catch you up.

Roy What?

Louise gestures that she wants to have a word with Bev

Roy catches on and exits UR, *rolling up his newspaper and slipping it into the back pocket of his trousers as he goes*

Louise Listen. Friends?
Bev Of course.
Louise (*sitting next to Bev*) I didn't mean what I said about you last night.
Bev What did you say?
Louise You know ... about you not being family and that.
Bev Well I'm not.
Louise My mother likes you a lot ... and I get a bit jealous sometimes.

Pause

Bev I haven't got a mother.
Louise I know ... and I've got a mother and a half.

They both laugh

Bev When you find her, tell her to come back.
Louise I'm happy to share her. She'll never be like a real mother to you ... but she can be a mother-in-law. (*She gets up and stands just outside the lounge door*)
Bev (*laughing*) Don't you start.
Louise (*for Darren's benefit*) I know you don't like Darren ... but tell me how much you hate him.
Bev (*loudly*) You don't want to know, Louise.
Louise (*even louder*) Yes I do.
Bev (*louder still*) I hate his guts.
Louise Brill. I'll see you when we get back.

She rushes off R *to join Roy*

Bev looks at the ring Darren gave her last night

Darren enters from the bedroom, dressed. He walks through the lounge and stands at the door. He sees Bev outside

Darren There you are.
Bev There you are what?
Darren (*moving the radio out of the way as he sits down on the top step*) We've been wondering where you were.

Bev We?
Darren Me and Louise. Haven't seen the old girl, have you?
Bev Not since breakfast, no.

Long pause

Darren (*uneasily*) About last night ... I gave you a ring, didn't I? I didn't
know what I was doing.
Bev We both didn't.
Darren It was the drink.
Bev I had too much as well.
Darren It was a stupid thing to do.
Bev The drink?
Darren The ring.

Pause

Bev We were only messing about.
Darren (*going to her*) That's right ... it was just a laugh really ... wasn't it?
Bev Course. Neither of us were serious.

She tentatively offers him the ring and he tentatively takes it

It's no big deal, we had a couple of drinks together, that's all.
Darren We did more than get drunk.
Bev I'm the one who should be saying, "My God, what did we do last night"?
Darren So why aren't you then?
Bev Perhaps I don't regret it, like you.
Darren I didn't say I regretted it.
Bev Oh come on.
Darren I didn't.
Bev I probably disappointed you.
Darren No you didn't.
Bev Well you disappointed me.

He looks at her

You fell asleep.
Darren I fell asleep?

She doesn't answer

Before or after?

Bev During.
Darren Oh ... no I didn't ..
Bev Believe me I've got no reason to lie.
Darren That's awful.
Bev It's bloody terrible!

Pause

Darren Listen, you won't tell anyone, will you?
Bev (*going to him*) Well it's not something I'm likely to blurt out, is it? I mean it doesn't say much for my ego either. Either way you've ruined my reputation.
Darren What can I say?
Bev At best, nothing. Better if we both put the whole thing behind us.
Darren Can you do that?
Bev I'm going to try.
Darren It's not going to be easy for me.
Bev Of course it's not. Your old ego has just taken one hell of a knock, hasn't it?
Darren Well it's different for a bloke.
Bev Says a bloke.
Darren It is.
Bev Deal with it how you want, Darren ... (*She raises her voice*) Your secret's safe with me.
Darren Oh don't let's have a row. I had enough with the one last night.

A pause. They look at each other and Bev eventually sits back down. After a moment he turns one of the chairs around and sits, facing her

The old man doesn't think she was kidding ... You know, about her not having the treatment ... What do *you* think?
Bev She *sounded* pretty serious. And you know your mother, Darren ... when she's made her mind up it's going to be very difficult to get her to change it.

Pause

Darren Listen, are you coming back to our house after dinner today?
Bev No, I'm staying down till Tuesday. I've got to paint the van.
Darren (*looking at the van*) On your own?
Bev Well there's no-one else ... unless you're offering to help.
Darren Oh, why would I want to do that?

Bev (*imitating his voice*) Oh, I don't know, Darren. It's a big job. I just
thought you might like to help. (*Frustrated with him, she stands*) What's
the matter with you? There's no ulterior motive in it.
Darren No?

Bev turns to walk off, L

Where are you going?
Bev (*stopping*) To get a newspaper, if you must know.
Darren Make it the *Wales on Sunday* then?

Bev stomps off

Suddenly, Louise is heard crying and wailing off. Louise and Roy enter, R.
*Louise is beside herself. She is holding Marlene's shell suit close to her
chest. Roy is carrying a pair of woman's shoes*

Roy (*trying to calm her*) No no ... I'm sure they're not your mother's.
Louise (*crying helplessly*) It is, it is hers, I know it is.
Roy She had it from the market, mun — there must be thousands like that.
Louise (*screaming*) It's Mammy's I'm telling you.
Roy (*holding up the pair of shoes*) And I've never seen these before in my
life.
Louise She had them new to come down here.
Roy Are you sure?
Louise (*screaming*) I was with her when she bought them.
Darren What's going on?
Louise Oooh, Da. It's Mammy.
Darren What's the matter with her?
Louise She's gone. (*She sits down*) She's gone and ... she's gone and done
herself in. (*She cries again*)
Darren (*kneeling beside her*) Done herself in ... How do you know?
Louise We found her clothes on the beach. She's walked in the sea and
drowned herself.
Roy No, I don't believe it, me. I mean there was no note — nothing.
Louise When I think of what she said last night ——
Darren She wouldn't do something like that. Not Mammy.
Louise She said she wasn't going to have the treatment, didn't she? You
heard her.
Darren So you think she's gone and drowned herself instead.
Roy I can't believe it, I can't. I mean she wouldn't go off and do something
like that without saying something, mun.

Louise Well she's hardly going to say, "Wash and wipe the dishes, Louise ... oh and by the way, I'm just going down the beach to drown myself", now would she?

Darren What was the last thing she said this morning?

Louise Well she could hardly speak to me.

Darren Or me. What about you, Dad?

Roy She was a bit quiet, I'll admit that.

Louise What did she say to you?

Roy Last like, before she went?

Darren and Louise nod

(*Thinking*) I can't remember.

Darren Come on, Dad, it's important.

Roy I wasn't taking a lot of notice.

Louise Well did she say something like, "So long ..." or, "Look after the kids". Or anything like that?

Roy (*thinking about it*) We were having a cup of tea by here. (*He sits down in a chair*) And I think she said something like, "That Louise can be a bit of a cow when she wants to" — and then she went.

Darren Didn't you ask her where she was going?

Roy Well no. I mean you don't, do you.

Louise (*standing, outraged*) A bit of a cow? Mammy said I was a bit of a cow?

Darren Now you know you can be.

Louise (*turning on Darren*) What about you? You said far more to her last night than I did. If she's done anything to herself it's because of you not me.

Roy Hang on — wait a minute. Where's Bev? I bet they've met up and gone off shopping somewhere.

Darren No they haven't. I was with Bev just now. She hasn't seen her.

Louise (*sitting and crying again*) I want my mother.

Roy Perhaps we'd better look for a life-guard or something.

Louise cries even louder

Darren Good idea, yes. Come on, let's go and find him. I don't know where to look though ... do you remember seeing anybody on the beach?

Roy No. (*He has an idea*) Come on — we'll ask the man at the gate.

He exits, DR

Darren Come on, Louise.

Darren and Louise follow Roy off

A pause

Bev enters L *with a* Wales On Sunday *newspaper*

Bev (*calling*) Darren! I've got your *Wales On Sunday*.

There is no response

Suddenly Marlene runs on, R. *She is wearing a black T-shirt, denim jacket, a miniskirt and a pair of Doc Martens. She rushes to get into the caravan unseen but is spotted by Bev*

Marlene (*laughing hysterically*) Now before you say anything, I haven't looped the loop. These rags aren't mine — I borrowed them off the beach.
Bev From who?
Marlene I don't know ... but some Hell's Angel is going to have to go home in my shell suit, love.
Bev What happened?
Marlene I don't know. I fancied a dip so I took my clothes off and went in the sea. When I came out some silly bugger had pinched my clothes. I wasn't going to walk all the way back here in my bathing suit so I helped myself to these. (*She looks down at the clothes*) Mind you, I think I'd have been less conspicuous if I'd walked home naked.
Bev You don't like your new look then?
Marlene Thinking about it, I reckon they must belong to that woman.
Bev What woman?
Marlene What's her name, now? You know, she's got shops everywhere.

Bev cracks up laughing

What are you laughing at now?
Bev Sue Ryder!
Marlene That's the one.
Bev Marlene, you're a girl and a half.
Marlene I know, and that half is spilling out over everything. (*She goes up the lounge steps*) I'd better change before Roy sees me.
Bev He might like it.
Marlene That's what I'm afraid of, love. Oooh hey, you haven't got a camera, have you?
Bev In the van.

Marlene Take my photo. Should be good for a laugh, what do you think?

Bev quickly gets a camera from just inside the kitchen door

Bev Who are you going to show it to?

Marlene I'll show it to my grandchildren. I'll keep it on the mantelpiece — frighten 'em away from the fire. (*She laughs*)

Bev (*kneeling, getting into position*) You haven't got any grandchildren.

Marlene No I know, and from what I hear about Wayne, I haven't got much chance, either. (*She holds her finger in the air then curls it towards the floor*)

Bev Your hopes don't improve much with Darren.

Marlene What's that?

Bev Nothing. Smile!

Marlene Wait a minute — let me get the pose right. (*She bends her knees, picks up the bottom of the T-shirt as if it was a dress and puckers up her lips — Marilyn Monroe style*)

Bev takes the photo and it immediately pops out of the front of the camera

Oh my God! It's one of them pulverized ones.

Bev takes the picture from the camera and hands it to Marlene. She puts the camera under the barbecue

Marlene They're marvellous today, aren't they? Do you know, if my mother could raise her head now she wouldn't believe it. She thought electricity was a miracle, see. We take a hell of a lot for granted nowadays mind, don't we?

Bev Television.

Marlene Motor cars.

Bev Medicine.

Marlene Toilet roll. (*Suddenly she screams with laughter. The photograph has developed*) Oh my God! Get a look at this. Talk about toilet roll, I look as though I've shit myself by here.

Bev (*hysterically*) I don't know about the mantelpiece, Ma — I'd burn it if I were you.

Marlene Oooh you got to have a laugh see, haven't you? I'm going to get changed, before I get to like it. Come and give me a hand, will you?

Marlene and Bev go inside the van and exit into the bedroom

Roy and Louise enter from behind the van, R. Roy is still holding Marlene's shoes

Roy Well it's a mystery to me, I'll tell you that now. I've never know a beach without a life-guard, have you?

Louise Perhaps we should report her to the police.

Roy They won't want to know, mun. She hasn't been gone long enough.

Louise I know, but when we tell them the circumstances. What do you think, Da? (*She turns to him but he's not there. Calling*) Darren? He was behind us a minute ago.

Darren races on, UR

Darren I was talking to that couple. They said they've seen her.

Roy There you are!

Louise Have they?

Darren They said she was walking along the main road wearing a miniskirt, T-shirt and Docs.

Louise That doesn't sound like Mammy to me.

Roy Or me ... (*He sits down*) I wouldn't mind having a look at her though all the same.

Louise hits him on the back

Darren They were sure it was her.

Pause

Roy You don't think it's that HRT do you?

Darren I don't know. What's HRT?

Roy Something to do with hormones, i'n' it?

Louise It effects women different ways.

Roy It wouldn't make your mother dress up in a miniskirt though, would it?

Darren Look, what are we going to do? Are we going to report her to the police ——?

Louise (*sitting*) That's what I said.

Darren Or should we give it another hour and see if she turns up?

Roy I still can't believe any of all this, me.

Darren Let's go and sit in the van and go over it again.

Louise I think that's a waste of time, Da.

Darren Look Louise, I don't want to have to say this but Mammy's been missing for the best part of an hour. If she wanted to top herself she'd have done it by now.

Louise (*crying*) If she has gone and killed herself I'll never speak to her again.

Roy thinks about what Louise has said. He thinks it sounds a bit odd but he can't work out why

Darren What are you thinking, Dad?

Roy I was just wondering ...

Darren What?

Roy What HRT means.

Louise I feel so helpless.

Darren (*sitting*) There's not a lot we can do.

Louise What do you *really* think has happened to her, Da?

Darren I think she's killed herself.

Louise She should never have come down here.

Darren *We* shouldn't have you mean.

Louise Yeah, it's all our fault.

Darren I'm to blame mostly. I gave her the most grief.

Roy I still don't think she's done it.

Louise I wasn't very nice to her either, remember. We're all to blame really. You too, Dad.

Roy Me? What have I done?

Darren It's what you haven't done.

Louise You've never made a fuss of her.

Roy Hey! I gave her you two, didn't I?

Darren When was the last time you put your arms around her?

Pause

Roy Last night if you must know.

Louise (*crying*) Oh there's lovely.

Roy It gets cold in that van in the early hours.

Darren We've never shown her how we really feel.

Roy *You* have.

Louise (*crying*) And now it's too late.

Darren No I haven't. We can't seem to do that in our family. It must be in the blood.

Louise Speak for yourself. I've always been one for touching.

Roy And me.

Pause

Darren Things are going to be awful without her, you know that, don't you?

Roy It doesn't bear thinking about.

Louise And even though you said some awful things to her last night, Da, I don't want you taking all the blame yourself.

Darren I wasn't going to.

Louise I'll have my share as well.

Roy Wait a minute, wait a minute—I've just thought of something ... What's going to happen to me?

Louise What do you mean?

Roy Well ... if what you're saying is ... you know, right — and your mother has gone and ... you know ... where do I fit in?

Darren Who's going to look after you, you mean?

Roy Exactly.

Louise You're going to have to look after each other.

Darren He can't look after me. He needs Mammy to tell him when to change his underpants.

Roy And what about our ironing?

Louise Don't look at me, Mammy's been doing mine for weeks.

Roy Oh God ... let's face it, we're going to be in a right bloody hole, aren't we?

Darren Look, we'll be all right. We're just going to have to pull together as a family.

Louise I don't think we should be talking like this now. (*She crys again*) Not when Mammy's probably floating ... face down out there somewhere.

Roy (*reflecting*) I told her when we were courting to learn to swim.

Marlene and Bev enter from the bedroom. When they hear Darren speak they stop inside the van to listen

Darren When I think of all the things we never said to her.

Louise We all took her for granted, didn't we?

Darren I meant what I said last night, you know ... but I'd take it all back today.

Louise I just want to put my arms around her and tell her I'm sorry.

Marlene (*yelling*) Well you can if you want to, love, I'm not stopping you. (*She comes to the door*)

All hell breaks loose. Louise is hysterical and rushes to Marlene, followed closely by Darren and Roy. Roy puts Marlene's shoes down on the chair

Louise Oh Mam, what happened? Where have you been?

Marlene Only for a dip, love. What's it all about? (*She takes her shoes from the chair and sits down*)

Darren (*to Bev*) You said you didn't know where she was.

Bev I didn't at the time.

Louise We found your clothes on the beach. We couldn't see you anywhere and we thought ——

Marlene (*slipping the shoes on*) — I had done away with myself.

Roy I knew you hadn't done it, sweetheart!

Darren Me and Lou didn't know what to think.

Louise We even went looking for a life-guard.

Bev There isn't one.

Marlene Story of my life, love.

Darren (*to Bev*) We know that now.

Marlene Well well, so you thought I'd popped my clogs, did you?

Darren We've been through hell this last hour.

Marlene Good enough for you ... talking to your mother like that last night. Still, if you want to say you're sorry.

Darren What? (*He moves away*)

Marlene If you want to put your arms around me and tell me you didn't mean it ...

Louise (*resting her arm on Marlene's shoulder*) Go on, Da, you said you wanted to.

Darren Yeah, but that was when I thought she was dead.

Marlene Well pardon me for breathing.

Darren I can't take back what I said or my life won't be worth living. She practically runs it for me now.

Marlene Well your grief didn't last long.

Darren As long as I thought you were dead.

Marlene So nothing's changed then? Everything is exactly as it was last night?

Louise Course it isn't. You should have seen him here earlier on — I don't know who was crying the most — me or him.

Marlene That'll be the day when he sheds a tear over me.

Louise It's true, isn't it, Da? (*She makes a face at him in order to get him to agree*)

Darren I can't take back what I said last night, right, 'cause I meant it. No-one's arranging my love life for me. And when I get married — if I get married, it'll be to someone I choose, not anyone else.

Roy Oooh come on, sweetheart — let's go for a pint before you cook dinner.

Roy exits R. Marlene trots after him

Louise (*to Darren*) You've gone and messed it all up now, haven't you?

Darren What?

Louise We're never going to get her to ... oh never mind.
Bev What's going on?
Louise We're worried about my mother ... Darren was wondering ——

Darren pushes Louise in the back before storming off into the van and exiting into the bedroom

(*Shouting after him*) He's like a big kid sometimes.

Pause. Bev gets the bag of charcoal out of the top step of the van, and Louise sits down

He likes you a lot.
Bev You've got to be joking.
Louise It's true. I've known him a long time ... and you like him too, don't you ...? Come on — you can tell me.

Bev begins to prepare the barbecue

Bev (*loudly, for Darren's benefit*) He's all right.
Louise Admit it, you know you like him.

She doesn't answer

Tell him. It'll be a lot easier then.
Bev I'm the least of his problems.
Louise The trouble with Darren is if he'd met you outside the family he probably would have asked you out anyway ... he's fighting against it now because he knows it's what my mother wants. If she would only leave you both alone ——
Bev Now you know she can't do that. (*She wipes her hands with a towel from the shelf under the barbecue. She picks up the camera, puts it round her neck and moves near to Louise*)
Louise She did the same with me and Wayne. I was much more of a push-over though.

Pause. Bev sits next to Louise

This thing about the treatment. She's got to go through with it. If she's serious about not having it ... would you have a word?
Bev (*putting her hand on Louise's leg*) It's not my place, Louise.
Louise What about if Darren asked you?

Bev Oh he wouldn't do that ... would he?

Louise (*getting up and heading for the lounge door*) You leave him to me.

Bev What are you going to do?

Louise (*turning round*) I don't know ... but something's got to be done. Mammy's got to get her treatment, and you've got to get together with Darren — if only to find out it doesn't work between you.

Bev You're getting to sound like your mother.

Louise Why not? I am her daughter after all.

Louise strikes a similar pose on the top step of the van as her mother did earlier. Bev holds up the camera and takes a shot of it

The Lights change. Tom Jones sings "My Mother's Eyes"

Louise goes into the van and exits into the bedroom. Bev picks up the tray of tea things and exits into the bedroom as well, using the other door

Darren enters from the bedroom carrying a tray of uncooked pork chops. He walks straight out to the barbecue. He places the tray underneath and proceeds to light the barbecue. Bev follows him out, sits in one of the chairs and reads the newspaper. Marlene also enters from the bedroom, followed by Louise and, lastly, Roy

The Lights revert and the music fades

Marlene fusses at the stove, Louise takes half a sliced loaf, breadboard, butter and knife from one of the cupboards and hands them to Roy, who sits at the table and starts to butter the bread. Smoke billows up from the barbecue

Bev (*going to Darren*) Let me give you a hand with that.

Darren I can manage.

Bev Let me help you.

Darren I'm fine, mun!

Bev God, you're really scared, aren't you?

Darren Of what.

Bev Me.

Darren (*laughing*) You've got to be joking.

Bev Well, not of me personally. Of what you think I represent.

Darren And what's that?

Bev Commitment. I know you like me but I scare you shitless. I'm not going to eat you up then spit you out through the gap in my teeth.

Darren Promise?

Bev If I offer help it's not some coded message meaning I fancy you and I want you to take me to bed.

Darren Any more than me refusing you means any more than you refusing me.

Bev Good. (*Not sure what all that means*) Well, I'm glad we've got that sorted out of the way.

Marlene (*standing at the lounge door*) I hope you're keeping an eye on those chops, Darren.

Darren makes a face

Now, I've got the potatoes on, Louise is washing the salad and Roy is buttering the bread.

Bev What can I do?

Marlene You can give him a hand cook the meat.

Bev He said he can manage.

Marlene Don't you believe it, love. The only thing he's ever cooked is his goose. (*She winks and goes back into the van*) Make sure there's no greenfly on that lettuce now, Louise, there's a good girl.

Pause

Bev (*to Darren*) I'm curious. Why did you come back here last night after saying you were going home?

Darren It didn't have anything to do with you.

Bev Oh good God no, can't have me thinking that, can we?

Darren It didn't.

Bev Answer me then.

Darren I changed my mind, that's all. I had some thinking to do so I had a couple of pints in a pub.

Bev Thinking's all right, but sometimes it's better to talk ... Why would I think you stayed because of me?

Darren I don't know. I just want to make it absolutely clear, that's all. I don't want any misunderstanding.

Bev Of course — wouldn't it be awful if I read all the wrong signs.

Darren Look, you wanted to know why I changed my mind and I've told you. There was nothing more to it than that ... now do you understand?

Bev Yes. You're coming across perfectly clear.

Darren I hope I'm not coming across at all.

Bev Figure of speech.

Marlene How the hell could you miss a caterpillar that size, Louise?

Pause

Bev (*sitting in one of the chairs*) You haven't half got an ego on you, haven't you?

Darren What are you talking about?

Bev What makes you think for one minute I'd be interested in someone like you? Just because your mother thinks it's a wonderful idea to pair us up, but I don't. I'm just as embarrassed at what she's trying to do as you are.

Darren Are you?

Bev Yes ... well ... no. I'm not, actually. I think it's all a bit of a laugh.

Darren Pardon me if I don't join in.

Bev Look, Darren — we are two very strong individual people with minds of our own. Your mother's not going to make either of us do anything we don't want to, and watching her try is funny sometimes. (*She laughs*) Look at the lengths she made poor old Roy go to last night just to get us both to stay down here.

Darren (*going to her*) I don't think it's funny, right? I think it's sad.

Bev She loves you very much.

Darren Oh sure. So that's why she's decided not to have treatment ... for the undying love of her kids.

Bev She could easily be talked out of that.

Darren Not by me.

Bev I could try.

Pause

Darren Would you?

Bev But I'm the wrong person. You're her two eyes.

Darren (*kneeling beside her*) I wouldn't know what to say to her.

Bev You wouldn't have to say anything. All you'd have to do is put your arms around her and tell her you're sorry.

Darren For what? I haven't done anything.

Bev And neither has she. Look, Darren — if anything happens between us — or if anything *doesn't* happen it'll be because of us and have nothing to do with your mother at all. She hasn't got any influence on us ... she only thinks she has ... but it's no big deal. Now I can handle that ... can't you?

Louise comes out of the kitchen door

Louise Hope I'm not interrupting anything.

Darren Now don't *you* start.

Louise (*going to them*) What are you talking about?

Darren We were just saying that because you left Wayne all on his tod last night, he probably took someone back to the house and spent the night with her. (*He goes back to the barbecue*)

Louise (*following him*) Oh very funny.

Darren I would have.

Louise Well Wayne's not you ... thank God. (*She hits him*)

Bev (*going to Darren*) You wouldn't have ... would you — in Wayne's position?

Darren (*looking over at Louise before answering*) Yeah.

Bev hits Darren in the same spot as Louise did. Roy continues to butter the bread. Marlene gets cutlery out of the drawer

Roy What time we leaving, sweetheart?

Marlene We'll go straight after dinner.

Roy No, I mean tomorrow. I need to know, to book a taxi.

Marlene Well my appointment's for ten o'clock.

Roy (*holding the knife up playfully*) Aha!

He has caught her out. She was going to have her treatment all along. Marlene realizes she's been had and makes a face

Bev (*to Louise*) No need to worry any more about your mother — Darren's got it sorted.

Darren Have I?

Louise (*to Bev*) I thought you were our best shot.

Bev No, Darren's our trump card, I'm sure.

During the following, Bev and Louise get two more folding chairs out from under the van and put them up

Roy So you are going to have your treatment after all then.

Marlene Well ay. Only don't go telling them yet though. Let 'em sweat it out a bit first.

Louise (*to Darren*) What are you going to say to her?

Bev It's not so much the words ... it's the action, isn't it, Da?

Darren flags Bev with the barbecue utensil. Bev and Louise sit down next to each other

Roy I thought you wasn't serious when you said it.

Marlene Oh I was at the time ... but then I thought ... I can't just give in. I'm a fighter, me. I won't rest till all the ends are tied up.

Roy What you mean?
Marlene Well, I'm used to having my own way, aren't I?

Roy looks at her

   I want to see our Darren settled ... and if I can't swing it this year, I'd better
   make sure I'm around *next* August.
Roy Why don't you leave them to get on with it. If it happens it happens.
Marlene I don't leave anything to chance, me. Nothing grows 'less you
   water it.
Roy You want to be careful you don't drown the bloody pair of 'em. (*He
   finishes buttering the bread and proceeds to cut it from corner to corner*)
Marlene (*looking through the window*) Look at our Louise out there now.
   Why the hell doesn't she leave them alone. (*She calls her through the
   window*) Louise, come and salt these potatoes, there's a good girl.
Louise (*going to Darren*) Well I'd like to think Wayne thought too much of
   me to go and do something like that.
Darren He's a fella whose had two or three drinks over the top and whose
   wife has walked out on him in a night club. Who's to say what he'd get up
   to. (*He bumps her out of the way with his hip*)
Bev I'm sure he's no different to the rest of the valley boys, Louise. (*This is
   meant for Darren*) They're all mouth and crotch ... but the minute you say,
   "Yeah all right, come on then", they run — in the opposite direction.
Marlene (*at the kitchen door*) Louise! Go and sort out the cutlery out, will
   you — there's a good girl.

*Louise goes inside through the lounge door. Marlene comes outside. Louise
sits at the table opposite Roy. He finishes cutting the bread and places the
triangular pieces in a pyramid shape on the breadboard*

Marlene (*going to Darren at the barbecue*) Now then — how are those
   chops doing?
Darren They're fine — how's yours?
Marlene (*snatching the utensil out of his hand*) You're not letting them burn
   now, are you?
Darren If you wanted to cook them why did you give them to me?
Marlene I just didn't want the two of you to get carried away talking and
   forget about them, that's all.
Darren Liar. That's exactly what you wanted.
Marlene Now why would I want you to burn the chops?
Darren That's not what I meant.
Marlene (*shoving the utensil back into his hand*) Now then, Bev, where are
   we going to eat, out here or in there?

Bev Out here. The table's at the back of the van and we've put the chairs out.

Marlene Right. Do us a favour, Da?

Darren (*under his breath*) Put the table out.

Marlene Put the table out.

Darren (*getting it and placing it* C) You are speaking to me then?

Marlene Well ay. Pointless quarrelling, i'n' it?

Darren That's what *I* think.

Marlene Life's too short for that. Now, the 'tatoes are boiling, so dinner should be on the table in quarter of an hour.

Bev What time you leaving?

Marlene Straight after dinner. Soon as I've washed up and put away, you know.

Bev On no you're not. That's my job. I'm doing that.

Marlene (*laughing*) Can't wait to see the back of us, eh?

Bev Enjoyed it then have you, Ma?

Marlene (*sitting down next to Bev*) Oh it's been a marvellous weekend, love ... marvellous. And I was determined to get down here, see.

Bev (*smiling*) I know you were. You can come and stay down any time, you know that, don't you?

Marlene Can I?

Bev If ever you and Roy fancy a break.

Marlene Hey I might hold you to that.

Bev I'm sure you will, Marlene.

Marlene How about next weekend?

Pause

Bev Well I want to paint the van.

Marlene I thought you were doing that this week.

Bev It's a couple of days work. Especially for one. It'll probably take me three weekends altogether.

Roy comes out of the van and begins to walk off, R

Marlene Why don't you have some help then? (*She nods in Darren's direction*)

Bev It's not easy to find, Marlene.

Marlene (*seeing Roy, shouting*) Oi!

Roy freezes

(*Standing*) Where are you off to?

Roy I'm going to phone Wayne.
Marlene What do you want phone Wayne for?

Pause

Roy I don't know.
Louise (*from just inside the lounge door*) He's ringing him for me.
Marlene Why the hell don't you ring him yourself then?
Louise Because I'm not speaking to him.
Marlene Well if you're not speaking to him why do you want your father
    to phone?
Louise I want to know if he's in the house, right? I couldn't cope if I rang
    and someone else answered. Go on now, Dad. And hurry up, dinner won't
    be long.
Roy (*turning to go then turning back*) What have I got to say to him again
    now if he answers?
Louise Just ask to speak to me.
Marlene (*shouting*) How the hell can he do that!
Louise Now look, Mam, I know what I'm doing. (*To Roy*) Just ask to speak
    to me right, and when he says I'm not there and that he thought I was with
    you, tell him you haven't seen me.
Roy What do I say if someone else answers?
Louise Well if it's a fella ask to speak to Wayne, if it's a girl hang up and lie
    to me.
Marlene (*sitting back down*) I wish you'd stop playing games, the pair of
    you.
Darren She can't do that, mun. It's a family trait, didn't you know? (*He goes
    into the van and gets three plates, two breakfast bowls and a table-cloth
    from out of the cupboard*)
Louise Hurry up, Dad.

    Roy turns and exits

    You think Wayne would have come looking for me, wouldn't you?
Marlene Look here, I left your father once ... (*Shouting after him*) And he
    didn't come looking for me either.
Louise How did you get back together then?
Darren (*coming out of the van*) They haven't, didn't you notice? (*He lays
    the table*)
Marlene I took the pair of you with me to my sister's, stayed there and slept
    on the bed settee for three weeks. And then one day I woke up and thought ...
    "Why the hell am I here and he's at home in a double bed?" So I went back
    ... chucked him out instead.

Louise But why did you chuck him out?

Darren 'Cause when she got there he wasn't in bed by himself.

Marlene That's not true ... your father's never looked at another woman ... I know because he's never looked at me. Well not hard anyway.

Darren Just as well.

Marlene (*threateningly*) Watch it now, will you?

Darren Only joking. (*He goes to Marlene*) You're a cracker for your age.

Marlene Don't waste it on me.

Darren It's true. (*He stands behind her, puts his arms around her and kisses her head*) You're the best-looking mother I've got.

Marlene I know what you're up to and it's not going to work.

Darren I don't know what you're talking about.

Marlene (*getting up and going into the van through the kitchen door*) I'm not having chemotherapy, Darren, and that's an end to it!

Darren (*calling after her*) Mam!

Marlene (*calling back*) No!

Pause

Darren Well I've done my bit, it's up to somebody else now.

Marlene sits down at the kitchen table and reads a newspaper. Pause. Darren goes to the barbecue

Bev You know, the more I think about it the more I think she's bluffing.

Darren And me.

Louise (*going to Darren*) But we can't afford to take the chance.

Darren I knew me talking to her wouldn't work.

Bev reads the Wales On Sunday

Louise Well what else are we going to do, 'cause we just can't leave it.

Darren You try.

Louise I don't think I'm the one. (*Quietly*) And it's not fair to ask Bev. Even though I'm sure she stands the best chance.

Darren It doesn't matter how fair it is as long as it works. Ask her.

Louise It would be better coming from you.

Darren Are you kidding? She doesn't even like me.

Louise Ask her.

Darren What if she says no.

Louise (*insisting*) Ask her.

Louise goes to the top step of the kitchen steps. She turns to Darren and nods her head towards Bev. Darren is reluctant but eventually obliges. As he approaches Bev she looks up from the paper. Darren stops in his tracks. He is speechless. He makes a silly laugh and returns to the barbecue. Louise gives up and goes into the van

Marlene (*putting her paper down*) I suppose you've come in to talk me round now, have you?

Louise Would it do any good?

Marlene Not a lot ...

Louise turns away, disappointed

   (*Whispering*) I've changed my mind anyway.

Louise (*turning*) Oh Mam! (*She sits next to her*)

Marlene Shut up now, I don't want them to hear.

Louise You're definitely going to go through with it then?

Marlene Keep it to yourself, I'll handle it my way.

Louise Who else knows?

Marlene If I play my cards right I might be able to pull this off after all. (*She points to Darren and Bev outside the van*) Remember now — not a word to anyone.

Louise Why?

Marlene 'Cause it'll spoil everything, that's why.

Louise grabs hold of her and gives her a hug

   Hey, come on now. Dry those couple of glasses for me by there, will you?

Louise Tea-towel?

Marlene In the drawer. There's a clean one.

Louise (*standing*) I'm glad and everything, but what I want to know is why you changed your mind? (*She doesn't wait for Marlene's answer, but turns and opens the drawer. She takes out a small rubber article*)

Marlene Well, it doesn't matter how hurt and disappointed you are ... when the chips are down, something inside you rallies round. It's easy enough to give up and give in but I've always liked a challenge, me.

Louise What's this? (*She holds it up to one eye*) An eye bath.

Marlene (*jumping out of the seat and rushing to her*) Er, you dull bugger, it's a cap.

Louise A what?

Marlene A Dutch cap.

Louise You mean ——

Marlene The contraceptive. Yes.

Disgusted, Louise throws it away from her and it lands on top of the bread and butter

Don't throw it on the bread and butter, Louise. We know where it's been.
Louise (*picking it up with her thumb and forefinger*) Whose is it do you think?
Marlene Well I'll tell you for nothing, love — it's not mine.

Wondering how it fits, Louise lowers it in that direction. Marlene slaps her hand

Louise What's it doing in with the tea-towel?
Marlene Search me. Ask Bev.
Louise Is it hers?
Marlene Well it's hardly any bugger else's. (*She opens the drawer behind her*) Put it back in the drawer now and we'll say nothing, that's best ...

Before Louise has a chance to do this, Marlene closes the drawer again

No, on second thoughts. Put it in your bag.
Louise What?
Marlene Stick it in your handbag and we'll take it home with us.
Louise We can't do that, what if she ——
Marlene Exactly!

Pause

Louise Hang on. You've still got the problem of keeping Darren down here.
Marlene You leave that to me, love. I've got something up my sleeve.
Louise Even if he stays, you can't be sure she'll need this. (*She holds up the cap*)
Marlene Look, love. If a couple of bottles of wine, a starry night and the sea air doesn't stir things, nothing will.
Louise Perhaps we should bring Wayne down here.
Marlene Yes love, perhaps we should. (*She points to the cap*) The bag.

Marlene exits into the bedroom

Louise puts the cap into her bag before getting three glasses out of the cupboard. Darren leaves the barbecue, turns a chair back to front and sits by Bev. Pause

Darren Louise thinks it might be a good idea if you had a chat to the old girl.
Bev What do *you* think?
Darren She might take more notice of you.
Bev Why?
Darren I don't know ... you're our best shot.
Bev Says who?
Darren We both think so ... So what do you think?
Bev (*folding the paper and putting it down*) Why is it so hard for you, Darren?
Darren What?
Bev You hate asking for anything. Well you hate asking me, anyway.
Darren It's nothing personal.
Bev I think it is. It's all right to owe a favour, you know.
Darren I don't like owing anyone anything.
Bev That's because you always think there's a price to pay.
Darren Well isn't there?
Bev So if I said I'd talk to your mother, what do you think would be *my* price?
Darren I don't know ... me?
Bev (*laughing*) You don't half love yourself, don't you?

Louise comes out of the van carrying squash and the glasses, which she sets on the table

Louise Everything's almost ready.
Bev I wish somebody would let me do something.
Darren (*going back to the barbecue*) Why don't you go and have a chat to the old girl.

Louise takes Bev by the arm and speaks confidentially

Louise Can you keep something to yourself?

Bev nods

She doesn't want anyone to know yet, but my mother's decided to go ahead with her treatment.
Bev Why?
Louise What does it matter as long as she's had a change of heart?
Bev No, I mean why doesn't she want anyone to know?
Louise I think she wants to tell everyone together. You won't say anything?
Bev Cross my bra and hope to die.
Louise Do us a favour. Bring out the salad.

Bev goes into the van

Darren (*to Louise*) Everything all right?
Louise (*pouring squash into the glasses*) You had a word then?

He nods

It's all working out fine.
Darren I just hope she can pull it off.
Louise I've got every confidence in her.

Roy enters DR

Louise Dad! What happened? (*She goes to him*)
Roy Nothing, love. He answered the phone — I said exactly what you told
me to and that was that.
Louise Didn't he sound worried?
Roy Oh he was beside himself. I could hear him biting his nails.
Louise Brill. This is just about ready. (*She goes into the van*)

*Marlene enters from the bedroom and goes straight over to the cooker and
the pan of boiling potatoes*

Roy (*to Darren*) Oi, come here.

Darren goes to Roy

Keep this to yourself now, right, but some piece answered the phone.
Darren What?
Roy I'm telling you — I rang the number and a girl answered.
Darren Wait till I get my hands on Wayne.
Roy Don't you say anything down here mind, right? That's my advice.
'Cause if Louise gets to know we'll have hysterics all the way home, and if
your mother catches wind of it ... she'll ruin Wayne first and ask questions
after.
Darren My lips are sealed.
*Roy goes into the van and sits at the table. Bev comes out with the bowl of
salad*

(*To Bev*) Hey, what do you think about Wayne?

She looks at him

    The old man rang the house now and a girl answered.

Bev Does Louise know?

Darren No, we're not going to say anything. You won't tell her, will you?

Bev Why should I?

Darren We've decided not to tell anyone.

Bev Why did you tell me then?

Darren (*for a split second he can't answer her and makes a silly laugh*) Did you have a word with the old girl?

Marlene comes out of the van. She is carrying the saucepan of potatoes

Marlene How are those chops, Darren, are they done?

Darren (*going back to the barbecue*) Just about.

Marlene (*dishing up at the table*) Now there's not enough cutlery to go round so some of you are going to have to eat with a spoon.

Darren How can I eat a pork chop with a spoon?

Marlene I'll cut it up for you, love, like I usually do.

Bev laughs

Darren Don't say that, she'll believe you.

Marlene It's true, Bev. He only stopped using a potty a year ago.

Bev laughs even louder. Roy comes out of the van carrying the breadboard

Darren Oh very funny.

Marlene (*handing a plate to Bev*) Tell him to put the meat on that.

Bev takes the plate over to Darren at the barbecue. Marlene continues to dish up the meal

Roy Where do you want me to sit, sweetheart?

Marlene You can sit anywhere.

Roy I thought you'd want it boy girl, boy girl.

Marlene (*putting the saucepan temporarily on the table*) This is a barbecue Roy, not a bloody dinner party. Sit where you like.

Roy moves to sit nearest to her

    Not there. Sit at the end.

Roy moves to the right end of the table, still holding up the bread and butter.
He is about to sit down

Not that end.

He sits at the other end and places the bread and butter on the table. Louise
comes out of the van with all the available cutlery. Bev holds the plate and
Darren places the chops on it

Darren They're lovely looking chops.
Bev I bet you say that to all the girls.
Darren I suppose you can't wait to see the back of us.
Bev Your mother and father are welcome down here any time.
Darren And me?
Bev I use the van myself most weekends.
Darren What does that mean?
Bev Work it out for yourself. (*All the chops are now on the plate and she takes*
     them over to the table) Pork à la charcoal grill.

Bev hands the plate of chops to Marlene who puts one chop on each plate

Marlene Oh hey, they look nice.
Darren (*going inside through the kitchen door*) Fancy a can, Dad?
Roy Ay, go on then.
Bev If I'd have been down here on my own now, look, I'd have only opened
     a tin of beans and sausage.
Marlene That's the trouble with you, my girl, you're not having enough tidy
     grub down you.
Bev (*slightly insulted*) Marlene!
Marlene Well you're not.
Bev I eat well.
Marlene Wouldn't think it to look at you.
Bev I'm overweight as it is.
Marlene Get out of it. There's more meat on a gypsy's dog. Sit by there,
     Louise. (*She points to the seat next to Roy*)

Darren comes out of the van with two lagers and hands one to his father

You go next to me, Darren — and you there, Bev.

They all sit

Oh that's nice, isn't it? Boy girl, boy girl. (*She sits down herself*) Tuck in now, everyone, I don't want to see anything left.

They all begin eating. Pause

Darren Can I borrow somebody's knife?
Louise How can you eat salad with a spoon?
Darren The same way as you eat a pork chop.
Marlene Just get on with it.

Pause

This is nice, isn't it? Shame Wayne isn't down here.
Louise Yeah — I bet he's worried sick. I can't wait to go home and make it up to him.

Roy and Darren share a look

Bev Yes, and better luck this time, Louise.
Darren What do you mean?
Bev (*to Louise*) Sorry.
Louise (*jumping in*) Nothing! Nothing, nothing, nothing, nothing. Nothing.
Marlene (*pointing with her knife*) It wouldn't be fair to tell you, Darren — it's girl talk. Something very private between me, Bev and Louise.

Louise looks down to continue her eating. Marlene lets the knife she is holding slide slowly until it points in a downward position. Darren immediately laughs and holds his finger up, but crookedly. Marlene gives him a dig in the ribs but Louise has seen everything. She pouts. Everyone tucks back into their lunch. A pause as everyone eats

I've been thinking.

Everybody stops eating and freezes

I've changed my mind. I still think my kids are a pair of selfish sods ... but I've changed my mind.
Darren About the treatment?
Marlene I was dead serious about it at the time, mind. I wasn't messing about.
Darren Why the change of heart then?

Marlene Well don't sound so bloody disappointed.

Darren I didn't, did I?

Marlene I've just come to the conclusion that it's pointless raising eighteen hundred pounds for a Macmillan bed only to end up in the bugger myself.

Roy Does that mean you're not going to bother with all that fund-raising then?

Marlene No indeed. I promised them a bed and that's exactly what they're going to get ... but don't worry I'm not going to ask any of you lot to help me.

Relieved, they all start eating again

I *was* going to ... but certain people — who shall remain nameless — have shown their true colours this weekend and I'm not going to simple myself to ask.

Pause

I was going to ask you, Roy, to do that sponsored drink. That would have brought in a good couple of hundred. I was going to ask you, Darren, to do a sponsored snooker match. And you, Louise ... (*She sits up straight and smiles*) Well it would have been nice for *you* to do something for *me* for a change. But there you are ... at the end of the day, you can't live my life for me and I can't live yours for you.

Darren That's my girl.

Marlene If ever I've interfered in the past ——

Darren What do you mean if?

Marlene (*slamming down her cutlery*) If ever I've interfered in the past it's only because I've known better. But from now on though, I'm going to let you make your own mistakes.

Pause

Which reminds me. Louise, have you got that cap safe?

Roy What cap?

Marlene Oh ... (*She improvises madly*) My cap. I bought in the shop yesterday. Yes. To wear round the house when my hair falls out. (*To Louise*) Well?

Louise Yeah, I got it in my bag.

Darren What makes you think we'll make mistakes?

Marlene Oh you will. I'm banking on you making a big bugger.

Darren Like what?

Marlene I'd tell you, Darren — but as you know I've finished interfering, love.

Louise Well this is great, isn't it? You've changed your mind, you're having your treatment, so everything's all right after all.

Marlene And as soon as we get home after tea, we'll have a tidy drink to celebrate.

Roy We'll be home before tea, mun.

Marlene Shut up, Roy.

Darren But we will.

Marlene No we won't. Bev's been good enough to let us have this van for nothing. She had planned to paint it this weekend but we've messed all that up.

Bev No you didn't.

Marlene Shut up, Bev.

Louise I hope you're not going to suggest what I think you're going to suggest.

Marlene For God's sake ... shut up, will you, Louise. With five of us at it it'll only take a couple of hours.

Bev No you can't do that, Marlene.

Marlene Why not?

Bev I've only got two brushes.

Marlene Well that's all right, *I'll* stay down and do it with you.

Darren You can't do either — you're going into hospital tomorrow.

Marlene Well Louise can't do it, she's got to go back home to put things right with Wayne, and — (*referring to Roy*) he can't do it, 'cause he's only ever painted by numbers.

Darren This smells like a set up.

Marlene No. Now I've told you, I've finished interfering.

Bev I'm quite capable of painting the van on my own, Marlene.

Marlene I'm sure you are, Bev but you're not going to. Not this year, anyway.

Darren OK, I'll do it.

Marlene No, I'm not having you thinking I've had anything to do with it. No. Louise can take you two home and I'll stay down with Bev.

Louise But how are you going to get home? You can't go to the hospital in the morning from here.

Marlene Oh no ... Well I hadn't thought of that, look.

Darren It's all right I'll do it, I said.

Marlene I don't think so ... I'll never stop hearing about it.

Darren You will.

Marlene I'll have it for breakfast, dinner, tea and supper.

Darren You won't.

Marlene No, I'd rather do it myself.
Darren (*insisting*) I *want* to do it.
Marlene Good, that's settled then.

The agreement came so quick Darren almost didn't catch it

Bev (*to Darren*) Why?
Darren Why what?
Bev Why have you offered to paint the van?
Darren Well, one good turn ...
Bev What's that supposed to mean?
Marlene (*standing*) Let's have a toast.
Bev What, with squash?
Marlene Whatever. To the fund-raising.
Darren The what?
Marlene The fund-raising ... that I'm going to do ... on my own ... by myself ...
single-handed ... with nobody to help me.
Roy (*really insisting*) Now look there's no way you can take on something
like that on all by yourself.
Marlene (*affectionately*) And to Roy.
Roy Me?
Marlene Yes, 'cause I love 'im to bits.
Roy Why me?
Darren You sound like a victim.
Bev (*smiling*) Aren't we all?
Marlene Because if you hadn't had a bone in your throat these — (*referring
to Darren and Bev*) wouldn't have stayed down last night.
Darren He didn't *have* a bone in this throat.
Marlene Shut up, will you?
Louise (*standing*) To Bev, for letting you have the van.
Bev (*standing*) To Darren, for offering to help me paint it.
Darren (*standing*) To Louise for — (*he can't think of any good reason*) for
being Louise.

A slight pause; they all look to Roy

Roy Yeah, cheers everybody!
Louise Dad! It's your turn.
Roy For what?
Darren We all toasted somebody. It's your turn to toast Mammy.
Roy (*getting up*) I knew that, mun. I was only messing about.

They all hold up their drinks. Pause

    I don't know what to say now.

Darren To the old girl?

Bev Who I'm sure is going to get a lot of help with the fund-raising?

Roy Ay. And who'd better be around for a long time to come.

Marlene Oh Roy ... that's the nicest thing you've ever said to me. Cheers
    everybody.

All Cheers!

*Tom Jones immediately blasts out, "You Are My Reason To Live". The Lights
fade a little, leaving the table in a pool of light. Black-out*

CURTAIN

FURNITURE AND PROPERTY LIST

ACT I

On stage: Caravan. *In it:*
    Benches
    Table
    Table seat. *In it:* duvet
    Cupboards. *In them:* tea-towels, cutlery, crockery, matches, bottle opener, nail file, wine glasses, peanuts, etc.
    Television (practical)
    Gas lamps
    Two ring gas cooker
    Sink
    Battery
    Water container (*in top step*)
    Bag of charcoal (*in top step*)
    Net curtain
    Wine bottle (*in bedroom*)
    Two glasses (*in bedroom*)
  Four chairs
  Barbecue
  Upturned milk-crate
  Small stones

Off stage: Twelve-pack of lager (**Roy**)
  Newspaper (**Roy**)
  Loaf of bread (**Bev**)
  Beach bag (**Darren**)
  Suitcase (**Darren**)
  Fish and chips, bottle of pop, etc. (**Bev** and **Darren**)
  Telephone receiver (**Bev**)
  Telephone receiver (**Darren**)
  Wine (**Bev**)

Personal: **Marlene**: watch
  Bev: handbag containing sun-tan lotion
  Louise: handkerchief
  Darren: ring

ACT II

Set: Portable radio
Tea-pot, cups, etc.
Camera
Barbecue. *Under it:* towel
Tray of uncooked pork chops (*in bedroom*)
Newpaper
Salad, breadboard, bread, butter, knife, squash, cutlery, crockery, table
    cloth, etc.
Two folding chairs (*behind van*)
Table (*behind van*)
Dutch cap

Off stage: Toilet roll (**Roy**)
Newspaper (**Roy**)
Towel (**Bev**)

LIGHTING PLOT

Exterior and interior settings
Practical fittings required: gas lights in van

ACT I

To open: Full stage lighting; bright, sunny morning effect

Cue 1   **Darren** and **Bev** exit   (Page 6)
          Change to indicate passage of time

Cue 2   The **company** freeze   (Page 10)
          Coloured pools of light; then black-out

Cue 3   When ready   (Page 11)
          Full stage lighting

Cue 4   **Marlene** and **Roy** exit into the bedroom   (Page 15)
          Crossfade; bring up two pools of light L *and* R *for
          telephone scene*

Cue 5   The dial tone sound stops   (Page 16)
          Change lighting to cover **Darren** *and* **Bev** *moving* C

Cue 6   **Darren** exits into the bedroom   (Page 16)
          Revert to previous full stage lighting

Cue 7   **Marlene** and **Bev** exit into the bedroom   (Page 20)
          Fade lighting

Cue 8   Tom Jones sings "I'm Never Going to Fall in Love"   (Page 20)
          Bring up evening effect when ready

Cue 9   **Marlene**: " ... and off up into the sun."   (Page 23)
          Car lights approaching then switch off

Cue 10	**Louise**: " ... you know what she's like." *Car lights approaching*	(Page 27)
Cue 11	**Marlene**: "... our banger to me." *Car lights snap off*	(Page 28)
Cue 12	Tom Jones sings "My Foolish Heart" *Crossfade to late evening effect; a starry night*	(Page 33)
Cue 13	**Roy** turns off gas lights in the kitchen *Snap off kitchen gas light and covering spot*	(Page 33)
Cue 14	**Louise** turns off gas lights in the lounge *Snap off lounge gas light and covering spot*	(Page 33)
Cue 15	Tom Jones sings "I Can't Stop Loving You" *Black-out*	(Page 37)

ACT II

To open:	Full stage lighting; bright, sunny morning effect	(Page 38)
Cue 16	**Bev** takes a photo of **Louise** *Lighting change; early evening effect*	(Page 54)
Cue 17	Tom Jones sings "You Are My Reason to Live" *Lights fade to pool, then Black-out*	(Page 72)

EFFECTS PLOT

Throughout, there is the sound of the birds singing and the crash of waves

ACT I

Cue 1	When ready after opening Car approaches and pulls up; three car doors slam	(Page 1)
Cue 2	Coloured pools of light on stage *Tom Jones sings "Boney Maloney"; fade when ready*	(Page 10)
Cue 3	**Bev**: "Don't you *dare* hang up!" *Dial tone; cut off when receivers are replaced*	(Page 15)
Cue 4	**Marlene**: " What do you mean now?" *Car starts up and pulls away*	(Page 20)
Cue 5	The Lights fade *Tom Jones sings "I'm Never Going to Fall in Love"; fade when ready*	(Page 20)
Cue 6	**Marlene**: " ... and off up into the sun." *Car approaches and pulls up*	(Page 23)

Cue 7	**Louise**: " ... you know what she's like."	(Page 27)
	Car approaches and pulls up	
Cue 8	**Marlene**: ..."sounds like our banger to me."	(Page 28)
	Two car doors slam, off	
Cue 9	**Bev** exits	(Page 33)
	Tom Jones sings "My Foolish Heart"; fade when **Bev** *kicks the chair*	
Cue 10	There is a slap, off	(Page 37)
	Tom Jones sings "I Can't Stop Loving You"	

ACT II

Cue 11	At opening	(Page 38)
	Tom Jones sings "The Resurrection Shuffle"; to emanate from the portable radio when **Louise** *starts exercising; cut when* **Darren** *switches the radio off*	
Cue 12	The Lights change	(Page 54)
	Tom Jones sings "My Mother's Eyes"; fade when ready	
Cue 13	**Roy** sits at the table	(Page 54)
	Smoke starts to billow up from barbecue	
Cue 14	**All**: "Cheers!"	(Page 72)
	Tom Jones sings " You Are My Reason To Live"	